# Super Easy Ninja Slushi Cookbook for Beginners

# Super Easy Ninja Slushi Cookbook for Beginners

*Make Over 105 Refreshing and Delicious Frozen Slushy Treats with Simple Tips & Tricks*

**Leonard McGrane**

# Contents

# INTRODUCTION

There is something universally magical about a slushie. It's not just a drink; it's an experience—a frosty blend of flavor, fun, and nostalgia that can instantly brighten any moment. From childhood memories of sipping vibrant slushies on warm summer days to discovering gourmet creations with exotic ingredients, slushies have a special place in our hearts. This book is here to help you recreate those moments and craft new ones, right from the comfort of your kitchen.

With the rise of the Ninja Slushi maker, achieving the perfect slushie texture has never been easier. This powerful machine turns ordinary beverages into extraordinary treats, allowing you to experiment with everything from fresh fruit juices to creamy frappes and even spirited cocktails. The possibilities are endless, and this book is your companion on this frosty adventure.

# Getting Started

At the heart of this cookbook lies the powerhouse that transforms everyday ingredients into frosty, delightful masterpieces: the Ninja Slushi Maker. With its powerful motor, precision settings, and sleek design, it takes the guesswork out of making slushies and turns the process into an effortless experience. The Ninja Slushi Maker is not just a kitchen gadget; it's a game-changer for anyone who loves creative beverages.

Here is some basic information to know about the Slushi machine:

1. The Ninja Slushi maker comes with multiple preset functions that allow you to easily create a variety of frozen drinks, from classic slushies to spiked beverages and frappes. Each preset is tailored to the type of drink you're making, ensuring optimal results with just the press of a button.

*Presets*

SLUSH: Ideal for classic slushies made with ice, fruit, or juice.

SPIKED SLUSH: For making slushies with alcoholic ingredients (like margaritas and frozen cocktails).

FROZEN JUICE: Designed for frozen juice slushies using frozen juice cubes or fresh juice.

FRAPPES: Great for creamy frappes, often made with coffee, milk, or other creamy ingredients.

MILKSHAKES: Perfect for creating indulgent milkshakes with ice cream and milk.

The recipes in this cookbook will be divided into these categories.

2. The Ninja Slushi maker comes with a built-in dispensing spout for easy and mess-free serving. The spout allows you to pour your slushie directly into glasses without any spillage or drips, keeping things neat and tidy. Once your slushie is ready, simply position your glass under the spout and pull the lever to dispense the slush.

3. The Ninja Slushi machine is designed for versatility, and the time required to prepare a drink varies depending on key factors:

Ingredients: Different compositions, such as juice versus soda, freeze at varying rates.

Volume: Larger quantities take longer to process than smaller ones.

Starting Temperature: Pre-chilled ingredients significantly reduce preparation time.

Typically, the process takes between 15–60 minutes. The machine beeps 3 times to signal readiness, but if your slushie reaches the desired texture earlier, you can dispense it immediately for enjoyment!

4. One of the standout features of the Ninja Slushi machine is its ability to maintain your slushie's perfect temperature for up to 12 hours. This capability ensures that your drinks stay icy, refreshing, and ready to serve long after they're prepared. To take full advantage of this, avoid frequent openings and only dispense the drink when ready to preserve its texture.

## Tips for Best Usage

o   Use Pre-Chilled or Frozen Ingredients

The Ninja Slushi maker performs best when ingredients are already cold or partially frozen. This not only ensures quicker processing but also gives your slushies a smoother, more consistent texture. For fruit-based recipes, freeze fresh fruit chunks before you blend. If using liquid ingredients like juice or milk, chill them in the fridge for a few hours.

o   Avoid Overfilling the Vessel

While the machine's capacity is generous, overfilling it can lead to uneven blending or spillage. Always keep the ingredients below the "MAX" line to allow the paddle to rotate freely. Leave a little extra space for blending especially when using carbonated beverages, as they can foam up during processing.

o   Colorful and Layered Slushies

Creating layers adds a wow factor to your slushies and makes them visually appealing for parties.

*Steps for Stunning Layers:*

Make Separate Batches: Blend each layer separately, using different colored juices, fruits, or syrups for distinct hues.

Chill between Layers: Allow each layer to freeze slightly in the glass or preferably, let it chill in the refrigerator before adding the next one to maintain distinct separation.

Use Contrasting Colors: Pair colors like red (strawberries) with green (kiwi) or orange (mango) with purple (blueberries) for vibrant visuals.

Gently Pour: Use a spoon or a tilted glass to carefully pour each layer to avoid mixing.

- o Use the Correct Preset for Each Recipe

The preset functions are tailored to different types of slushies, so selecting the right one ensures optimal results. Follow the recipe's guidance on which preset to use. For example, the "SPIKED SLUSH" setting is calibrated for alcohol-based drinks, while the "MILKSHAKE" preset works best with creamy blends.

- o Add Sweeteners Carefully

Too much sugar or syrup can make your slushies overly thick or sticky, affecting the texture and performance of the machine. Use natural sweeteners, like honey or agave nectar, in moderation. Strictly follow the exact quantity for each recipe.

- o Avoid Large or Hard Ice Cubes

The Ninja Slushi maker is powerful, but oversized or very hard ice cubes can strain the motor. Opt for smaller cubes or preferably utilize the blender for smoother operation.

- o Creative Presentation

The way you serve your slushie can make it even more enjoyable.

Decorate the Glass: Rim your glass with sugar, salt, or crushed candy for added flair.

Use Fun Glassware: Serve slushies in mason jars, tall glasses, or novelty cups for variety.

Garnish Artfully: Add a fruit skewer, edible flower, or drizzle of sauce for a gourmet touch.

Add a Straw: Brightly colored or patterned straws add a fun and functional element to your presentation.

- o Store Leftovers Correctly

If you make more slush than needed, store the leftovers in an airtight container in the freezer. When ready to enjoy again, let it thaw slightly and reprocess in the machine to refresh the texture.

- o Clean Immediately After Use

Cleaning your Ninja Slushi maker right after use prevents sticky residue from forming and keeps the components in top condition. Disassemble the parts and rinse them with warm water before washing. For tougher residues, soak the vessel and paddle in soapy water for a few minutes before scrubbing.

By following these tips, you'll not only make the most out of your Ninja Slushi maker but also enjoy consistently delicious frozen drinks.

# SLUSH

1. Honeydew Mint Slushie

2. Kiwi Strawberry Slushie

3. Mango Pineapple Slushie

4. Grape Slushie

5. Cherry-Limeade Slushie

6. Cucumber Melon Slushie

7. Blueberry Lemon Slushie

8. Watermelon Mint Slushie

9. Orange Creamsicle Slushie

10. Strawberry Lemon Slushie

11. Cucumber-Mint Slushie

12. Raspberry Lemonade Slushie

13. Mango Slushie

14. Citrus Fizz Slushie

15. Pineapple Coconut Slushie

16. Peach Slushie

17. Iced Tea Lemonade Slushie

18. Pomegranate Iced Tea Slushie

19. Peach Iced Tea Slushie

20. Mango Iced Tea Slushie

21. Sugar Free Lime Seltzer Slushie

22. Sour Lemon Lime Slushie

# Honeydew Mint Slushie

## Ingredients

- 2 cups honeydew melon (peeled, deseeded, and cubed)
- 1 tablespoon fresh mint leaves
- 2 tablespoons honey (optional, for added sweetness)
- 1 cup cold water

**Prep**: 5 minutes

**Servings**: 2

## Instructions

1. In a blender, combine the honeydew melon, mint leaves, and honey with the cold water. Blend until smooth.
2. Place the blended mixture in the refrigerator for 10-15 minutes to chill.
3. Pour the chilled mixture into the Ninja slushi maker. Turn on the machine and select the SLUSH setting to let it process the mixture.
4. Once the slushie is ready (the machine will beep three times), pour it into glasses and garnish with a sprig of mint or a small slice of honeydew for presentation.

## Nutrients (Per Serving)

Calories: ~110 | Carbohydrates: 28g| Sugar: 23g | Protein: 1g | Fat: 0g | Fiber: 1g

**Tips:** For an extra minty flavor, muddle the mint leaves slightly before blending.

# Kiwi Strawberry Slushie

## *Ingredients*

- 2 kiwis (peeled and sliced)
- 1 cup fresh or frozen strawberries (hulled)
- 1 tablespoon honey or agave syrup (optional)
- 1 cup cold water

**Prep:** 5 minutes

**Servings:** 2

## *Instructions*

1. Combine the kiwis, strawberries, honey (if using), and cold water in a blender. Blend until smooth.
2. Transfer the blended mixture to the refrigerator and let it chill for 10-15 minutes.
5. Pour the chilled mixture into the Ninja slushi maker. Turn on the machine and select the SLUSH settin to let it process the mixture.
3. Once the slushie is ready (the machine will beep three times), pour it into serving glasses.
4. You can garnish with a strawberry slice or a kiwi wedge for an extra touch.

## *Nutrients (Per Serving)*

Calories: ~95 | Carbohydrates: 22g| Sugar: 18g | Protein: 1g | Fat: 0g | Fiber: 3g

**Tips**: If using frozen strawberries, you may skip the chilling step.

# Mango Pineapple Slushie

## *Ingredients*

- 1 cup fresh mango chunks (peeled and deseeded)
- 1 cup fresh pineapple chunks (peeled and cored)
- 2 tablespoons lime juice (freshly squeezed)
- 1 tablespoon honey (optional, for sweetness)
- 1 cup cold water or coconut water

**Prep:** 5 minutes

**Servings:** 2

## *Instructions*

1. In a blender, combine the mango chunks, pineapple chunks, lime juice, honey, and cold water or coconut water. Blend until smooth.
2. Transfer the blended mixture to a refrigerator and chill for 10-15 minutes.
3. Pour the chilled mixture into the Ninja slushi maker. Turn on the machine and select the SLUSH setting to let it process the mixture.
4. Once the machine beeps three times, indicating the slushi is ready, pour it into glasses.
5. Garnish with a pineapple wedge, a mango slice, or a small mint sprig for added flair.

## *Nutrients (Per Serving)*

Calories: ~120 | Carbohydrates: 30g | Sugar: 26g | Protein: 1g | Fat: 0g | Fiber: 2g.

# Grape Slushie

## Ingredients

- 2 cups seedless grapes (green or red, depending on preference)
- 1 tablespoon freshly squeezed lemon juice
- 1–2 tablespoons honey or sugar (optional, based on sweetness preference)
- 1 cup cold water

**Prep**: 10 minutes

**Servings**: 2

## Instructions

1. Combine the grapes, lemon juice, honey (or sugar), and cold water in a blender. Blend until the mixture is smooth.
2. If you prefer a smoother slushi, strain the blended mixture through a fine-mesh sieve to remove grape skins and any pulp.
3. Transfer the blended mixture to a refrigerator and chill for 10-15 minutes.
4. Pour the chilled mixture into the Ninja slushi maker. Turn on the machine and select the SLUSH setting to let it process the mixture.
5. Once the slushi is ready (the machine will beep three times), pour it into glasses.

## Nutrients (Per Serving)

Calories: ~90| Carbohydrates: 24g | Sugar: 21g | Protein: 0.5g | Fat: 0g | Fiber: 1g

**Tips**:

- ✓ For a sweeter slushi, use red or Concord grapes. For a tangier taste, opt for green grapes.
- ✓ Add a few mint leaves or a splash of sparkling water for a unique twist.

# Cherry-Limeade Slushie

## *Ingredients*

- 1 ½ cups fresh or frozen cherries (pitted)
- ¼ cup fresh lime juice (about 2 limes)
- 2 tablespoons honey or agave syrup (adjust to taste)

**Prep**: 10 minutes

**Servings**: 2

## *Instructions*

1. In a blender, combine cherries, lime juice, honey (or agave syrup), and cold water. Blend until smooth.
2. If the cherries aren't cold, refrigerate the blended mixture for 10-15 minutes to enhance the slush texture.
3. Transfer the blended mixture to a refrigerator and chill for 10-15 minutes.
4. Pour the chilled mixture into the Ninja slushi maker. Turn on the machine and select the SLUSH setting to let it process the mixture.
5. Once the slushi is ready (the machine will beep three times), pour it into glasses.
6. Garnish with a cherry and a slice of lime for presentation.

## *Nutrients (Per Serving)*

Calories: ~120 | Carbohydrates: 28g | Sugar: 23g | Protein: 1g| Fat: 0g | Fiber: 2g

# Cucumber Melon Slushie

## Ingredients

- 1 ½ cups honeydew melon (peeled, deseeded, and cubed)
- 1 cup cucumber (peeled and sliced)
- 1 tablespoon lime juice
- 1–2 tablespoons honey (optional, for sweetness)

**Prep**: 10 minutes

**Servings**: 2

## Instructions

1. Combine the honeydew melon, cucumber, lime juice and honey (if using) in a blender. Blend until smooth and all ingredients are fully combined.
2. Transfer the blended mixture to a refrigerator and chill for 10-15 minutes.
3. Pour the chilled mixture into the Ninja slushi maker. Turn on the machine and select the SLUSH setting to let it process the mixture.
4. Once the slushi is ready (the machine will beep three times), pour it into serving glasses.
5. Garnish with a slice of cucumber or melon for an elegant touch.

## Nutrients (Per Serving)

Calories: ~80 | Carbohydrates: 20g | Sugar: 16g | Protein: 1g | Fat: 0g | Fiber: 1g

# Blueberry Lemon Slushie

## Ingredients

- 1 ½ cups fresh or frozen blueberries
- ¼ cup freshly squeezed lemon juice (about 2 lemons)
- 2 tablespoons honey or agave syrup (optional, for added sweetness)

**Prep**: 5 minutes

**Servings**: 2

## Instructions

1. In a blender, combine the blueberries, lemon juice and honey (if using). Blend until smooth.
2. Transfer the blended mixture to a refrigerator and chill for 10-15 minutes.
3. Pour the chilled mixture into the Ninja slushi maker. Turn on the machine and select the SLUSH setting to let it process the mixture.
4. Once the slushi is ready (the machine will beep three times), pour it into glasses.

## Nutrients (Per Serving)

Calories: ~90 | Carbohydrates: 22g | Sugar: 18g | Protein: 1g | Fat: 0g | Fiber: 3g

**Tips**: Add a bit of lemon zest to the blender for a more vibrant citrus kick.

# Watermelon Mint Slushie

## Ingredients

- 3 cups watermelon (peeled, deseeded, and cubed)
- 1 tablespoon fresh mint leaves
- 2 tablespoons lime juice (freshly squeezed)
- 1–2 tablespoons honey (optional, for added sweetness)

**Prep**: 10 minutes

**Servings**: 2

## Instructions

1. In a blender, combine the watermelon cubes, mint leaves, lime juice and honey. Blend until smooth.
2. Transfer the blended mixture to a refrigerator and chill for 10-15 minutes.
3. Pour the chilled mixture into the Ninja slushi maker. Turn on the machine and select the SLUSH setting to let it process the mixture.
4. Once the slushi is ready (indicated by three beeps from the machine), pour it into glasses.
5. Garnish with a sprig of mint or a small wedge of lime for added flair.

## Nutrients (Per Serving)

Calories: ~90 | Carbohydrates: 23g | Sugar: 20g | Protein: 1g | Fat: 0g | Fiber: 1g

**Tips**: Muddle the mint leaves slightly before blending to amplify their aroma.

# Orange Creamsicle Slushie

## Ingredients

- 2 cups freshly squeezed orange juice (or high-quality store-bought orange juice)
- ½ cup vanilla Greek yogurt
- ¼ cup heavy cream (optional, for extra creaminess)
- 2 tablespoons honey or maple syrup (optional, for added sweetness)
- ½ teaspoon vanilla extract

**Prep**: 10 minutes

**Servings**: 2

## Instructions

1. In a blender, combine the orange juice, vanilla Greek yogurt, heavy cream (if using), honey or maple syrup and vanilla extract. Blend until smooth.
2. Transfer the blended mixture to a refrigerator and chill for 10-15 minutes.
3. Pour the chilled mixture into the Ninja slushi maker. Turn on the machine and select the SLUSH setting to let it process the mixture.
4. Once the machine beeps three times, indicating the slush is ready, dispense it into glasses.
5. Garnish with an orange slice or a dollop of whipped cream.

## Nutrients (Per Serving)

Calories: ~140 | Carbohydrates: 26g | Sugar: 22g | Protein: 4g | Fat: 4g | Fiber: 0g

## Tips:

- Substitute the heavy cream with coconut cream for a dairy-free option.
- Add a pinch of orange zest for an extra burst of citrus flavor.

# Strawberry Lemon Slushie

## Ingredients

- 2 cups fresh strawberries (hulled and halved)
- ¼ cup freshly squeezed lemon juice
- 2 tablespoons honey or sugar (optional, for added sweetness)

**Prep**: 5 minutes

**Servings**: 2

## Instructions

1. In a blender, combine the strawberries, lemon juice and honey or sugar (if using). Blend until smooth.
2. Transfer the blended mixture to a refrigerator and chill for 10-15 minutes. Pour the chilled mixture int the Ninja Slushi maker vessel.
3. Turn on the machine and select the SLUSH setting. Allow the Ninja slushi maker to process the mixtur until it reaches the desired slush consistency (the machine will beep three times when it's done).
4. Once the slushi is ready, pour it into glasses.

## Nutrients (Per Serving)

Calories: ~95| Carbohydrates: 24g | Sugar: 20g | Protein: 1g | Fat: 0g | Fiber: 3g

# Cucumber-Mint Slushie

## Ingredients

- 1 large cucumber (peeled, seeded, and chopped)
- 1 tablespoon fresh mint leaves
- 1 tablespoon honey or agave syrup (optional, for sweetness)

**Prep**: 5 minutes

**Servings**: 2

## Instructions

1. In a blender, combine the chopped cucumber, mint leaves and honey or agave syrup (if using). Blend until smooth.
2. Transfer the blended mixture to a refrigerator and chill for 10-15 minutes. Pour the chilled mixture into the vessel of the Ninja slushi maker.
3. Turn on the machine and select the SLUSH setting. Let the machine process the mixture until it reaches the desired slushy texture.
4. Once the slush is ready (the machine will beep three times), pour it into glasses.

## Nutrients (Per Serving)

Calories: ~50 | Carbohydrates: 12g| Sugar: 9g | Protein: 1g | Fat: 0g | Fiber: 2g

# Raspberry Lemonade Slushie

## Ingredients

- 1 cup fresh raspberries (or frozen if fresh isn't available)
- ½ cup freshly squeezed lemon juice (about 2 lemons)
- 1 tablespoon honey or sugar (optional, to taste)

**Prep**: 10 minutes

**Servings**: 2

## Instructions

1. In a small bowl, dissolve the honey or sugar into the lemon juice by stirring.
2. In a blender, combine the raspberries and lemon juice mixture. Blend until smooth.
3. Transfer the blended mixture to a refrigerator and chill for 10-15 minutes.
4. Pour the chilled mixture into the vessel of the Ninja slushi maker. Turn on the machine and select the SLUSH setting.
5. Once the machine beeps three times, signaling that the slush is ready, dispense into glasses.

## Nutrients (Per Serving)

Calories: ~90 | Carbohydrates: 23g | Sugar: 21g | Protein: 1g | Fat: 0g | Fiber: 3g

# Mango Slushie

## Ingredients

- 2 cups fresh mango (peeled, pitted, and chopped)
- 1 tablespoon fresh lime juice
- 1 tablespoon honey or agave syrup (optional, for added sweetness)
- ½ cup of ice

**Prep**: 5 minutes

**Servings**: 2

## Instructions

1. Add the chopped mango, lime juice and honey/agave syrup (optional) to a blender. Blend until smooth. If you'd like a thicker texture, add ½ cup of ice and blend again.
2. For an extra refreshing slush, chill the blended mixture in the refrigerator for 10 minutes.
3. Pour the chilled mixture into the vessel of the Ninja slushi maker. Turn on the machine and select the SLUSH setting.
4. Once the machine beeps (indicating the slush is ready), pour the slush into glasses.

## Nutrients (Per Serving)

Calories: ~110| Carbohydrates: 28g | Sugar: 24g | Protein: 1g | Fat: 0g | Fiber: 3g

# Citrus Fizz Slushie

## *Ingredients*

- 1 cup fresh orange juice (preferably freshly squeezed)
- ½ cup fresh lemon juice
- ¼ cup lime juice
- 2 tablespoons honey or sugar (optional, for added sweetness)
- 1 cup cold sparkling water (or soda water for extra fizz)

**Prep**: 5 minutes

**Servings**: 2

## *Instructions*

1. Squeeze the fresh orange, lemon, and lime juice into a pitcher or mixing bowl. Add honey or sugar to the citrus juices if you prefer a sweeter slush. Stir until the sweetener dissolves.
2. Pour the citrus juice mixture into a blender and add the cold sparkling water. Blend for a few seconds until well combined.
3. Chill the blended mixture in the refrigerator for 10 minutes.
4. Pour the chilled mixture into the vessel of the Ninja slushi maker. Turn on the machine and select the SLUSH setting.
5. Once the slush is ready (the machine will beep three times), pour it into glasses.

## *Nutrients (Per Serving)*

Calories: ~60 | Carbohydrates: 16g | Sugar: 14g | Protein: 0g | Fat: 0g | Fiber: 1g

## *Ingredients*

- 2 cups fresh pineapple (peeled, cored, and cubed)
- 1 cup coconut milk (unsweetened or sweetened, based on preference)
- 1 tablespoon honey (optional, for added sweetness)

**Prep**: 10 minutes

**Servings**: 2

## *Instructions*

1. In a blender, combine the pineapple cubes, coconut milk, honey, and cold water. Blend until smooth.
2. Chill the blended mixture in the refrigerator for 10 minutes. Pour the chilled mixture into the vessel of the Ninja slushi maker.
3. Turn on the machine and select the SLUSH setting. Let it process the mixture until it forms a smooth, icy slush.
4. When the slushie is ready (the machine will beep three times), pour it into glasses.

## *Nutrients (Per Serving)*

Calories: ~140| Carbohydrates: 32g | Sugar: 28g | Protein: 1g | Fat: 4g | Fiber: 2g

# Peach Slushie

## Ingredients

- 2 cups fresh or frozen peach slices
- 1 tablespoon fresh lemon juice
- 1 tablespoon honey (optional, for added sweetness)

**Prep**: 10 minutes

**Servings**: 2

## Instructions

1. In a blender, combine the peach slices, fresh lemon juice, and honey (if desired). Blend until smooth.
2. Chill the blended mixture in the refrigerator for 10 minutes. Pour the chilled mixture into the vessel of the Ninja slushi maker.
3. Turn on the machine and select the SLUSH setting. Let the machine process the mixture until it forms a smooth, icy slush.
4. Once the slush is ready (the machine will beep three times), pour it into glasses.

## Nutrients (Per Serving)

Calories: ~80 | Carbohydrates: 22g | Sugar: 18g | Protein: 1g | Fat: 0g | Fiber: 2g

## *Ingredients*

- 1 cup brewed iced tea (strong, chilled)
- 1 cup freshly squeezed lemonade (chilled)
- 1 tablespoon honey or sugar (optional, for sweetness)

**Prep:** 10 minutes

**Chill Time:** 5 minutes

**Servings:** 2

## *Instructions*

1. Brew a strong cup of iced tea using your preferred tea (black or green works best). Let it cool completely, or preferably chill in the refrigerator.
2. In a blender, mix the chilled iced tea, lemonade, and honey or sugar (if desired). Blend until well combined.
3. Pour the chilled mixture into the vessel of the Ninja slushi maker.
4. Turn on the machine and select the SLUSH setting. Let it process the mixture until it forms a smooth, icy slush.
5. Once the slushie is ready (the machine will beep three times), pour it into glasses.

## *Nutrients (Per Serving)*

Calories: ~50| Carbohydrates: 13g | Sugar: 10g | Protein: 0g | Fat: 0g | Fiber: 0g

# Pomegranate Iced Tea Slushie

## Ingredients

- 1 cup freshly brewed and chilled green tea
- 1 cup pomegranate juice
- 2 tablespoons honey (optional, for added sweetness)

**Prep:** 10 minutes

**Servings:** 2

## Instructions

1. Brew a cup of green tea and allow it to cool completely. For faster results, refrigerate the tea for 10–1? minutes.
2. In a blender, mix the chilled green tea, pomegranate juice, and honey (if desired). Blend until smooth.
3. Pour the chilled pomegranate iced tea mixture into the Ninja slushi maker. Turn on the machine an? select the SLUSH preset.
4. Once the slushie is ready (the machine will beep three times), pour it into glasses.
5. Add a few fresh pomegranate seeds or a sprig of mint for decoration.

## Nutrients (Per Serving)

Calories: ~90 | Carbohydrates: 22g | Sugar: 18g | Protein: 0g| Fat: 0g | Fiber: 0g

## Ingredients

- 1 cup brewed and chilled peach-flavored tea (unsweetened or lightly sweetened)
- 1 cup fresh or frozen peach slices
- 1 tablespoon honey or sweetener of choice (optional)

**Prep:** 10 minutes

**Servings:** 2

## Instructions

1. Brew a cup of peach-flavored tea and let it cool to room temperature. For quicker results, refrigerate the tea until chilled.
2. In a blender, combine the chilled peach tea, peach slices and honey (if desired). Blend until smooth.
3. Chill the blended mixture in the refrigerator for 10 minutes. Pour the chilled peach tea mixture into the Ninja Slushi maker.
4. Turn on the machine and select the SLUSH setting. Let it process until the mixture achieves the perfect slush consistency.
5. Once the slush is ready (indicated by three beeps), pour it into glasses.

## Nutrients (Per Serving)

Calories: ~60 | Carbohydrates: 15g | Sugar: 13g | Protein: 0g | Fat: 0g | Fiber: 1g

**Tips:**

- Use decaffeinated tea for a kid-friendly version or if you prefer less caffeine.
- For a stronger peach flavor, steep a few slices of fresh peach in the brewed tea while it cools.

# Mango Iced Tea Slushie

## Ingredients

- 1 cup brewed and chilled black tea (or green tea if preferred)
- 1 cup fresh mango chunks (or frozen mango)
- 1 tablespoon honey or sweetener of choice (optional)
- 1 tablespoon fresh lemon juice

**Prep:** 5 minutes

**Servings:** 2

## Instructions

1. Brew your tea of choice (black or green) and allow it to cool completely. For best results, place the brewed tea in the refrigerator to chill.
2. In a blender, combine the chilled tea, mango chunks, lemon juice, and honey (if using). Blend until smooth and well-mixed.
3. Place the blended mixture in the refrigerator for about 10 minutes to ensure it's cold before processing
4. Pour the chilled mixture into the Ninja Slushi maker. Turn on the machine and select the SLUSH setting to process the mixture.
5. Once the slush is ready (the machine will beep three times), pour it into glasses.

## Nutrients (Per Serving)

Calories: ~120 | Carbohydrates: 30g | Sugar: 25g | Protein: 1g | Fat: 0g | Fiber: 2g

# Sugar Free Lime Seltzer Slushie

## Ingredients

- 2 cups fresh lime juice (about 4-5 limes)
- 1 can (12 oz) sugar-free lime seltzer
- 1 tablespoon stevia or other sugar substitute (optional, for added sweetness)

**Prep:** 5 minutes

**Servings:** 2

## Instructions

1. In a blender, combine the fresh lime juice, sugar-free lime seltzer, and stevia (if desired for added sweetness). Blend to mix the ingredients together.
2. Place the mixture in the refrigerator for about 5-10 minutes to chill.
3. Pour the chilled lime-seltzer mixture into the Ninja slushi maker
4. Turn on the machine and select the SLUSH setting. Allow the machine to process the mixture.
5. Once the slushie is ready (indicated by three beeps), pour it into glasses and serve immediately.

## Nutrients (Per Serving)

Calories: ~10 (depending on the brand of seltzer and stevia used) | Carbohydrates: 2g| Sugar: 0g | Protein: 0g | Fat: 0g | Fiber: 0g

# Sour Lemon Lime Slushie

## Ingredients

- 1 cup freshly squeezed lemon juice (about 4-5 lemons)
- ½ cup freshly squeezed lime juice (about 4-5 limes)
- 2 tablespoons sugar (or adjust based on preferred sweetness)

**Prep:** 5 minutes

**Servings:** 2

## Instructions

1. In a small bowl or pitcher, combine the lemon juice, lime juice and sugar. Stir until the sugar is dissolved completely.
2. If you prefer your slush even colder, place the juice mixture in the refrigerator for 10-15 minutes.
3. Pour the chilled mixture into the Ninja Slushi maker. Turn on the machine and select the SLUSH setting to process the mixture.
4. Once the slush is ready (indicated by the machine beeping three times), pour it into glasses and serve.

## Nutrients (Per Serving)

Calories: ~40 | Carbohydrates: 10g | Sugar: 9g | Protein: 0g | Fat: 0g | Fiber: 0g

# A short message from the author

Hey there! How's the book treating you? I'm super curious to know what you think about it! Your thoughts can really make a difference.

Could you spare just a minute to jot down a quick review on Amazon? Even a few sentences would mean the world!

Simply click the link 🔗 or scan the QR code below and scroll down to get to the *'Write a customer review'* button to leave your review on Amazon

🔗 rebrand.ly/slush/LM

QR code

Thank you for taking the time to share your thoughts!

# KIDS' FAVORITES

23. Virgin Mojito Slushie

24. Rainbow Layer Slushie

25. Gummy Bear Slushie

26. Cotton Candy Slushie

27. Classic Soda Slushie

28. Tropical Punch Slushie

29. Fizzy Apple-Cinnamon Slushie

30. Peachy Keen Slushie

31. Berry Burst Slushie

32. Orange Cream Soda Freeze

33. Blue Raspberry Fruit Punch Slushie

## Ingredients

- 2 cups sparkling water (chilled)
- ¼ cup fresh lime juice (about 2–3 limes)
- 2 tablespoons granulated sugar (or honey, optional for sweetness)
- ¼ cup fresh mint leaves (loosely packed)
- Optional garnish: lime wedges, mint sprigs

**Prep:** 5 minutes

**Servings:** 2

## Instructions

1. In a blender, combine the lime juice, mint leaves, and a small portion of the sparkling water (about ½ cup). Blend until smooth.
2. Pour the mixture through a fine sieve to remove mint pulp, if desired, for a smoother texture.
3. Place the strained lime-mint mixture in the refrigerator to cool for about 10-15 minutes.
4. Pour the chilled mixture into the Ninja slushi maker. Turn on the machine and select the SLUSH preset.
5. Let the machine process the ingredients until they form a smooth, icy texture.
6. Once the slushie is ready (the machine will beep three times), dispense it into glasses.

## Nutrients (Per Serving)

Calories: ~25 (without sugar or honey) | ~50 (with sugar) | Carbohydrates: 7g | Sugar: 5g | Protein: 0g| Fat: 0g | Fiber: 0g.

# Rainbow Layer Slushie

## *Ingredients*

- Red Layer: 1 cup strawberry juice or red fruit punch
- Orange Layer: 1 cup orange juice
- Yellow Layer: 1 cup pineapple juice
- Green Layer: 1 cup limeade or cucumber-lime juice
- Blue Layer: 1 cup blue raspberry drink (or a mix of clear soda with blue food coloring)
- Purple Layer: 1 cup grape juice
- Optional Garnishes: Whipped cream, colorful straws, or rainbow sprinkles

**Prep:** 5 minutes per layer

**Servings:** 2 large rainbow slushies

## *Instructions*

1. Ensure all the juices are chilled before starting. For each layer, use a separate small bowl for th respective juice or drink. Chill each juice for at least 10-15 minutes if not already cold.
2. Pour the first juice (e.g., strawberry juice for the red layer) into the Ninja slushi maker.
3. Select the SLUSH setting and let the machine process until the desired slushy consistency is achieved.
4. Carefully spoon the slush into a tall glass, ensuring it forms a solid base layer. Place the glass in th freezer while preparing the next layer to prevent mixing.
5. Rinse the Ninja slushi maker between each layer to avoid color blending.
6. Follow the same process for each juice, layering the slushies one by one (orange, yellow, green, blue, an purple).
7. Pour each new layer gently over the back of a spoon to maintain distinct layers.
8. Once the final layer is added, top with whipped cream, rainbow sprinkles, or a colorful straw if desired.

## *Nutrients (Per Serving)*

Calories: ~180 | Carbohydrates: ~45g | Sugar: ~40g | Protein: 1g | Fat: 0g | Fiber: 1g

**Tips:**

> ➤ You can use food coloring to adjust juice shades for a more vivid rainbow.
> ➤ Create your rainbow with fewer layers for a quicker version

*Ingredients*

- 1 cup gummy bears (plus extra for garnish)
- 1 cup lemonade or fruit punch (cold)
- 1 tablespoon grenadine syrup (optional, for added sweetness and color)

**Prep:** 10 minutes

**Servings:** 2

*Instructions*

1. In a small saucepan, add ½ cup of the lemonade or fruit punch and the gummy bears. Heat over low heat, stirring frequently until the gummy bears melt completely into the liquid.
2. Let the mixture cool to room temperature, or preferably place it in the refrigerator to chill.
3. Once the gummy bear mixture is chilled, pour it into the vessel of the Ninja slushi maker. Add the remaining lemonade or fruit punch and grenadine syrup (if using).
4. Turn on the machine and select the SLUSH setting to process the mixture.
5. Once the machine beeps three times, indicating the slush is ready, pour it into glasses.
6. Garnish with a handful of whole gummy bears.

*Nutrients (Per Serving)*

Calories: ~150 (depending on gummy bears and drink used) | Carbohydrates: 35g | Sugar: 30g | Protein: 1g | Fat: 0g | Fiber: 0g

# Cotton Candy Slushie

## *Ingredients*:

- 1 ½ cups cold cotton candy-flavored soda
- 1 tablespoon cotton candy syrup (available at most grocery stores or online)
- Optional: Whipped cream and a small piece of cotton candy for garnish

**Prep:** 5 minutes

**Servings**: 2

## *Instructions:*

1. Ensure the cotton candy-flavored soda is well-chilled. If not, place it in the refrigerator for at least 5-10 before starting.
2. Pour the cold soda and cotton candy syrup into the vessel of the Ninja slushi maker.
3. Turn on the machine and select the SLUSH preset to process the mixture.
4. Once the machine beeps three times, the slushie is ready. Dispense into glasses.
5. Top with a dollop of whipped cream and a small piece of real cotton candy for a magical presentation.

## *Nutrients (Per Serving):*

Calories: ~100 | Carbohydrates: ~25g | Sugar: ~22g | Protein: 0g | Fat: 0g | Fiber: 0g

## Ingredients:

- 2 cups of your favorite soda (e.g., cola, root beer, ginger ale, or lemon-lime soda)
- 1 tablespoon of fresh lime juice (optional, for added zing)

**Prep**: 5 minutes

**Servings**: 2

## Instructions:

1. Chill your soda in the refrigerator for 10-15 minutes.
2. Pour the chilled soda into the vessel of the Ninja slushi maker.
3. If you want a little extra tang, add fresh lime juice to the soda for a citrusy boost.
4. Select the SLUSH preset and let the machine process the soda mixture. The machine will beep three times when it's ready.
5. Once the slush is ready, dispense it into glasses.

## Nutrients (Per Serving):

Calories: ~100 (depending on the soda brand used) | Carbohydrates: ~27g | Sugar: ~25g | Protein: 0g | Fat: 0g | Fiber: 0g

# Tropical Punch Slushie

## *Ingredients*

- 1 cup tropical punch juice (store-bought or homemade)
- ½ cup pineapple juice (100% pure, unsweetened)
- ½ cup orange juice (freshly squeezed or store-bought)
- Optional: 1 tablespoon honey or agave syrup (for extra sweetness)

**Prep:** 5 minutes

**Servings**: 2

## *Instructions*

1. Combine the tropical punch juice, pineapple juice, orange juice, and honey/agave syrup (if using) in the Ninja slushi maker.
2. Turn on the machine and choose the SLUSH preset to process the mixture until it transforms into a smooth and icy slush texture.
3. Once the machine beeps three times to indicate the slush is ready, pour the slush into glasses.

## *Nutrients (Per Serving)*

Calories: ~120 I Carbohydrates: 28g I Sugar: 22g I Protein: 1g I Fat: 0g I Fiber: 1g

## Ingredients

- 1 ½ cups fresh apple cider or unsweetened apple juice
- ½ teaspoon ground cinnamon
- ½ cup sparkling water (apple-flavored or plain)

**Prep:** 5 minutes

**Servings:** 2

## Instructions:

1. In a small bowl, combine the apple cider (or juice) with ground cinnamon. Stir until the cinnamon is well blended with the juice.
2. Chill your apple-cinnamon mixture in the refrigerator for 10-15 minutes.
3. Pour the chilled mixture into the Ninja slushi maker.
4. Gently pour the sparkling water into the machine. This step ensures the slush retains its fizz.
5. Turn on the machine and choose the SLUSH preset to process the ingredients.
6. Once the machine beeps three times, indicating the slushie is ready, pour it into glasses.
7. Sprinkle a pinch of cinnamon on top or garnish with a cinnamon stick.

## Nutrients (Per Serving)

Calories: ~90 | Carbohydrates: 22g | Sugar: 20g | Protein: 0g | Fat: 0g | Fiber: 1g

# Peachy Keen Slushie

## Ingredients

- 2 cups fresh or frozen peach slices
- 1 cup orange juice (freshly squeezed or store-bought)
- 1 tablespoon honey or agave syrup (optional, depending on sweetness preference)

**Prep:** 10 minutes

**Servings:** 2

## Instructions

1. In a blender, combine the peach slices, orange juice, and honey or agave syrup (if desired). Blend until smooth.
2. Place the blended mixture in the refrigerator for about 5–10 minutes.
3. Pour the chilled mixture into the Ninja slushi maker.
4. Turn on the machine and select the SLUSH setting to process the mixture until it achieves a perfectly slushy texture.
5. Once the machine beeps three times, pour the slushie into glasses.

## Nutrients (Per Serving)

Calories: ~120 | Carbohydrates: 30g | Sugar: 24g | Protein: 1g | Fat: 0g | Fiber: 2g

# Berry Burst Slushie

*Ingredients*:

- 1 cup mixed berries (strawberries, blueberries, raspberries, blackberries; fresh or frozen)
- 1 tablespoon honey or agave syrup (optional, adjust for sweetness)
- 1 tablespoon fresh lemon juice

**Prep:** 10 minutes

**Servings**: 2

*Instructions*

1. In a blender, combine the berries, cold water, honey or agave syrup (if desired), and lemon juice. Blend until the mixture is smooth and all the berries are fully incorporated.
2. Transfer the blended mixture into a container and place it in the refrigerator for 10-15 minute to chill.
3. Pour the chilled berry mixture into the Ninja slushi maker vessel. Turn on the machine and select the SLUSH setting to process until the mixture.
4. Once the slush is ready (indicated by the machine beeping three times), pour it into glasses.

*Nutrients (Per Serving):*

Calories: ~60 | Carbohydrates: 14g | Sugar: 10g | Protein: 1g | Fat: 0g | Fiber: 3g

# Orange Cream Soda Freeze

## *Ingredients*:

- 2 cups orange soda (chilled)
- ½ cup heavy cream or half-and-half
- 1 tablespoon vanilla extract
- 1 tablespoon sugar (optional, for extra sweetness)

**Prep:** 5 minutes

**Servings**: 2

## *Instructions*

1. In a large mixing bowl, combine the chilled orange soda, heavy cream (or half-and-half), vanilla extract and sugar (if using). Stir until well combined.
2. For the best results, place the mixture in the refrigerator for 10-15 minutes to ensure it is cold.
3. Pour the chilled mixture into the Ninja slushi maker vessel.
4. Turn on the machine and select the SLUSH setting to process the mixture.
5. Once the machine beeps (indicating that the slush is ready), pour the slush into glasses.

## *Nutrients (Per Serving):*

Calories: ~150 | Carbohydrates: 34g | Sugar: 32g | Protein: 1g | Fat: 5g | Fiber: 0g

**Tips**: For a lighter version, you can substitute heavy cream with almond milk or coconut milk.

# Blue Raspberry Fruit Punch Slushie

## Ingredients

- 1 cup blue raspberry juice or drink mix
- 1 cup fruit punch
- 1 tablespoon fresh lemon juice
- 1–2 tablespoons sugar (optional, for added sweetness)

**Prep:** 10 minutes

**Servings:** 2

## Instructions

1. In a pitcher, combine the blue raspberry juice, fruit punch, and fresh lemon juice. Stir to mix evenly. If desired, add sugar to taste and stir until dissolved.
2. Place the mixed juices in the refrigerator for 10-15 minutes to chill.
3. Pour the chilled juice mixture into the Ninja slushi maker. Turn on the machine and select the SLUSH setting to process the mixture.
4. Once the slush is ready (indicated by three beeps), dispense it into glasses.

## Nutrients (Per Serving)

Calories: ~120 I Carbohydrates: 30g I Sugar: 26g

# SPIKED SLUSH

34. Classic Margarita Slush

35. Frozen Strawberry Daiquiri Slush

36. Piña Colada Slush

37. Frozen Mimosa Slush

38. Coconut Lime Daiquiri Slush

39. Slushy Tequila Sunrise

40. Hard Cider Slush

41. Watermelon Vodka Slush

42. Kombucha Slushie

43. Peach Bellini Slush

44. Pineapple Rum Punch Slush

45. Grapefruit Paloma Slush

46. White Wine Slush

47. Gin and Tonic Slush

48. Low Sugar Strawberry Margarita

49. Berry Sangria Slush

50. Espresso Martini Slushie

51. Rum and Coke Slush

52. Cinnamon Whiskey Cider

53. Mai Tai Slush

54. Aperol Spritz Slush

55. Boozy Banana Split Slush

# Classic Margarita Slush

*Ingredients*:

- 1 cup tequila (silver or your preferred type)
- ½ cup fresh lime juice (about 4-5 limes)
- ¼ cup orange liqueur (such as triple sec or Cointreau)
- 1 tablespoon simple syrup or agave nectar (optional, for added sweetness)
- Salt for rimming glasses (optional)

**Prep**: 5 minutes

**Servings**: 2

*Instructions*:

1. If you like a salted rim on your glass, rub a lime wedge around the rim of each glass, then dip them into salt.
2. In a pitcher or large bowl, mix all ingredients until properly combined.
3. Chill the mixture for 10-15 minutes
4. Turn on the Ninja slushi maker, select the SPIKED SLUSH preset to process the mixture.
5. Once the slush is ready (the machine will beep three times), pour it into the prepared glasses.
6. Garnish with a lime slice or wedge on the rim of the glass.

*Nutrients (Per Serving) (Approximate):*

Calories: ~150 | Carbohydrates: 7g | Sugar: 4g | Protein: 0g | Fat: 0g | Fiber: 0g

# Frozen Strawberry Daiquiri Slush

*Ingredients*:

- 1 ½ cups frozen strawberries
- 1 cup white rum
- ½ cup fresh lime juice (about 3-4 limes)
- 2 tablespoons simple syrup or agave nectar (optional, for sweetness)
- 1 tablespoon triple sec (optional, for added depth of flavor)

**Prep:** 5 minutes

**Servings**: 2

*Instructions*:

1. In a large mixing cup, combine the frozen strawberries, rum, lime juice, simple syrup (or agave nectar) and triple sec (optional).
2. Give it a stir to ensure everything is mixed.
3. Pour the prepared mixture into the Ninja slushi maker. Turn on the machine and select the SPIKEI SLUSH preset to process the mixture.
4. Once the slush is ready (the machine will beep three times), pour into glasses.

*Nutrients (Per Serving) (Approximate)*:

Calories: ~200 | Carbohydrates: 15g | Sugar: 12g | Protein: 1g | Fat: 0g | Fiber: 2g.

# Piña Colada Slush

*Ingredients*:

- 1 cup rum (white or coconut rum)
- ½ cup coconut cream or coconut milk
- 1 cup pineapple juice
- 2 cups frozen pineapple chunks
- 1 tablespoon simple syrup or honey (optional, for added sweetness)
- Pineapple slices or maraschino cherries (for garnish, optional)

**Prep**: 5 minutes

**Servings**: 2

*Instructions:*

1. In a blender, add the rum, coconut cream (or milk), pineapple juice, frozen pineapple chunks, and simple syrup (if using). Blend everything together to ensure it is smooth and well combined.
2. If you want your mixture extra cold, you can chill it in the refrigerator for about 10-15 minutes before processing.
3. Pour the mixture into the Ninja slushi maker. Turn on the machine and select the SPIKED SLUSH preset to process the mixture.
4. The machine will beep three times when the slush is ready.

*Nutrients (Per Serving) (Approximate):*

Calories: ~220 | Carbohydrates: 25g | Sugar: 20g | Protein: 1g | Fat: 12g | Fiber: 1g

# Frozen Mimosa Slush

*Ingredients:*

- 1 cup chilled champagne (or sparkling wine of your choice)
- 1 cup freshly squeezed orange juice
- 1 tablespoon orange liqueur (optional, for added flavor)
- 1 tablespoon simple syrup (optional, depending on sweetness preference)

**Prep:** 5 minutes

**Servings**: 2

*Instructions*:

1. In a pitcher, add the chilled champagne, fresh orange juice, orange liqueur (if using), and simple syrup (if you prefer a sweeter drink). Stir everything together to ensure it is well combined.
2. Turn on the Ninja slushi maker and select the SPIKED SLUSH preset to process the mixture.
3. The machine will beep three times to signal when the slush is ready.

*Nutrients (Per Serving) (Approximate):*

Calories: ~120 | Carbohydrates: 10g | Sugar: 9g | Protein: 0g | Fat: 0g | Fiber: 0g

# Coconut Lime Daiquiri Slush

*Ingredients*:

- 1 cup white rum
- ½ cup coconut cream (or coconut milk for a lighter version)
- ½ cup fresh lime juice (about 4 limes)
- 1 tablespoon simple syrup (optional, for added sweetness)

- Lime slices or wedges, for garnish (optional)

**Prep:** 5 minutes

**Servings**: 2

*Instructions*:

1. In a large pitcher or bowl, combine the white rum, coconut cream, lime juice, and simple syrup (if using).
2. Pour the prepared mixture into the Ninja slushi maker. Turn on the machine and select the SPIKED SLUSH preset to process the mixture.
3. The machine will beep three times to indicate it's ready. Pour the slushi into glasses.

*Nutrients (Approximate Per Serving):*

Calories: ~220 | Carbohydrates: 17g | Sugar: 14g | Protein: 1g | Fat: 7g | Fiber: 0g

**Tips**:

➢ For a lighter version, swap coconut cream for coconut milk to reduce the calorie count.
➢ You can also rim your glasses with a little salt or sugar for a fun twist on the classic daiquiri presentation.

## Slushy Tequila Sunrise

*Ingredients*:

- 1 cup tequila (silver or your preferred variety)
- ½ cup orange juice
- 1 tablespoon grenadine
- Orange slices or maraschino cherries for garnish (optional)

**Prep:** 5 minutes

**Servings**: 2

*Instructions*:

1. Pour the tequila and orange juice into the Ninja slushi maker vessel.
2. Turn on the machine and select the SPIKED SLUSH preset to process the mixture until it reaches a slushy consistency (the machine will beep three times when it's ready).
3. Dispense the slush into glass, now pour the grenadine into the glass. The grenadine will naturally settle at the bottom, creating the "sunrise" effect with the orange slushie on top.

*Nutrients (Per Serving) (Approximate):*

Calories: ~150 | Carbohydrates: 14g | Sugar: 12g | Protein: 0g | Fat: 0g | Fiber: 0g

Hard Cider Slush

*Ingredients*:

- 1 ½ cups hard cider (any variety you prefer)
- ½ cup apple juice (optional for added sweetness)
- 1 tablespoon lemon juice
- 1 tablespoon simple syrup (optional, adjust to taste)
- ½ teaspoon cinnamon (optional, for extra spice)

**Prep:** 5 minutes

**Servings:** 2

**Instructions**:

1. In a pitcher or mixing bowl, combine the hard cider, apple juice (if using), lemon juice, simple syrup (if desired), and cinnamon (optional). Stir the mixture well to combine all the ingredients.
2. Chill the mixture for 10-15 minutes in the refrigerator to speed up the slushing process.
3. Pour the chilled mixture into the Ninja slushi maker vessel. Turn on the machine and select the SPIKED SLUSH preset to process the mixture. The machine will beep three times when it's done.
4. Once the slush is ready, pour it into glasses. You can garnish with an apple slice or a sprinkle of cinnamon for extra flair.

*Nutrients (Per Serving):*

Calories: ~150 | Carbohydrates: 18g | Sugar: 16g | Protein: 0g | Fat: 0g | Fiber: 0g

**Tips**:

- Try adding a splash of ginger beer for a spicy kick or a small dash of nutmeg along with the cinnamon.
- Depending on the hard cider's ABV, the alcohol content of the slush will vary. Always drink responsibly!

Watermelon Vodka Slush

*Ingredients*:

- 2 cups frozen watermelon cubes
- ½ cup vodka (your preferred brand)
- ¼ cup lime juice (freshly squeezed)
- 1 tablespoon simple syrup or agave nectar (optional, for added sweetness)
- ½ cup cold water or club soda
- Fresh mint leaves for garnish (optional)

**Prep:** 5 minutes

**Servings**: 2

*Instructions:*

1. In a blender, combine the frozen watermelon cubes, vodka, lime juice, simple syrup (if desired), and cold water or club soda. Blend until smooth.
2. If you prefer an even colder slush, let the mixture sit in the refrigerator for 10-15 minutes.
3. Pour the chilled watermelon mixture into the Ninja slushi maker. Turn on the machine and select the SPIKED SLUSH preset to process the mixture.
4. Once the slushie is ready (you'll hear the machine beep three times), pour it into glasses. Garnish with a fresh mint sprig or a lime wedge for a finishing touch.

*Nutrients (Per Serving) (Approximate):*

Calories: ~120 | Carbohydrates: 15g | Sugar: 12g | Protein: 1g| Fat: 0g | Fiber: 1g.

Kombucha Slushie

*Ingredients*:

- 1 cup kombucha (flavored or plain, your choice)
- ½ cup vodka (or your preferred alcohol)
- 1 tablespoon honey or agave nectar (optional, for added sweetness)

- ½ cup fresh fruit (such as berries or citrus slices, optional for extra flavor)

**Prep:** 5 minutes

**Servings**: 2

**Instructions**:

1. In a large bowl or pitcher, combine the kombucha, vodka, and honey/agave nectar (if using). Stir to combine. If you're adding fresh fruit, blend the entire mixture to make it liquid.
2. Let the mixture sit in the refrigerator for 10-15 minutes
3. Pour the chilled mixture into the Ninja slushi vessel. Turn on the machine and select the SPIKED SLUSH preset to process the kombucha and vodka mixture.
4. The machine will beep three times once the slush is ready. Pour the kombucha slush into glasses and enjoy!

*Nutrients (Per Serving) (Approximate):*

Calories: ~120-150 (depending on alcohol content and any added sweeteners) | Carbohydrates: 10-15g | Sugar: 5-10g (depending on kombucha and any sweeteners used) | Protein: 0g | Fat: 0g | Fiber: 0g

## Peach Bellini Slush

*Ingredients*:

- 1 cup frozen peach slices
- ½ cup peach nectar or peach juice
- ¼ cup Prosecco (or your preferred sparkling wine)
- 1 tablespoon simple syrup or agave nectar (optional, for added sweetness)
- Fresh peach slices or mint for garnish

**Prep:** 5 minutes

**Servings**: 2

**Instructions**:

1.  Combine the frozen peach slices, peach juice or nectar, and syrup or agave nectar in a blender and blend to a smooth mixture.
2.  Place the mixture in the refrigerator for 10-15 minutes to chill. Add the chilled mixture to the Ninja slushi vessel.
3.  Turn on the machine and select the SPIKED SLUSH preset to process the mixture.
4.  Once the slush base is ready, pour in the Prosecco and give it a quick stir. Make sure to keep the carbonation intact by not overmixing.
5.  Dispense the peach bellini slushie into chilled glasses.
6.  Garnish with a fresh peach slice or a sprig of mint for a touch of elegance.

*Nutrients (Approximate, Per Serving):*

Calories: ~150 | Carbohydrates: 22g| Sugar: 18g | Protein: 1g | Fat: 0g | Fiber: 2g

Pineapple Rum Punch Slush

*Ingredients:*

-   1 cup pineapple juice
-   ½ cup white rum
-   ¼ cup coconut rum
-   ¼ cup orange juice
-   1 tablespoon grenadine
-   1 cup frozen pineapple chunks

- Lime wedges and mint leaves for garnish (optional)

**Prep:** 5 minutes

**Servings**: 2

*Instructions:*

1. In a blender or large mixing container, combine the pineapple juice, white rum, coconut rum, orange juice, grenadine, and frozen pineapple chunks. Blend to a smooth mixture.
2. For the best slush texture, refrigerate the mixture for 10-15 minutes before processing.
3. Add the chilled mixture into the Ninja slushi vessel. Turn on the machine and select the SPIKED SLUSH preset to process the mixture.
4. The machine will beep three times when the slush is ready, pour into glasses to enjoy.
5. Garnish with lime wedges and mint leaves for extra flair, if desired.

*Nutrients (Per Serving) (Approximate):*

Calories: ~200 | Carbohydrates: 28g | Sugar: 24g | Protein: 0g | Fat: 0g | Fiber: 1g

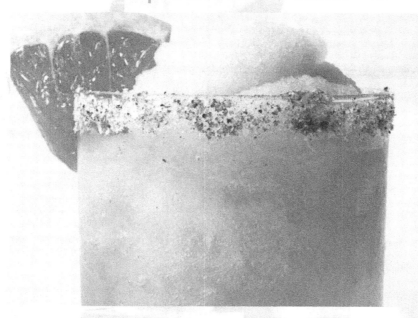

Grapefruit Paloma Slush

*Ingredients:*

- 1 cup tequila (silver or your preferred type)
- ½ cup fresh grapefruit juice (about 1-2 grapefruits)
- ¼ cup lime juice (about 2 limes)
- 1 tablespoon agave nectar or simple syrup (optional, for sweetness)
- ½ cup soda water or sparkling water
- Salt for rimming glasses (optional)

**Prep:** 5 minutes

**Servings**: 2

*Instructions*:

1. If you prefer a salted rim, rub a lime wedge around the rim of each glass. Then, dip the rim into a plate of salt to coat.
2. In a blender, combine the tequila, freshly squeezed grapefruit juice, lime juice, soda water, and ice cubes. Blend until smooth.
3. Pour the blended mixture into the Ninja slushi vessel. Select the SPIKED SLUSH preset to process the mixture.
4. Once the slush is ready (the machine will beep three times), pour it into your prepared glasses.

*Nutrients (Per Serving) (Approximate):*

Calories: ~150 | Carbohydrates: 10g | Sugar: 6g | Protein: 0g | Fat: 0g | Fiber: 0g.

White Wine Slush

*Ingredients*:

- 2 cups chilled white wine (a dry variety like Sauvignon Blanc or Pinot Grigio works best)
- ½ cup fresh lemon juice (about 2 lemons)
- ¼ cup simple syrup or honey (optional, for added sweetness)
- 1 cup frozen mixed fruit (such as berries, peaches, or pineapple)
- 1 tablespoon lemon zest (optional, for extra citrus flavor)

**Prep:** 5 minutes

**Servings**: 2

*Instructions*:

1. In a pitcher or bowl, mix the chilled white wine with the fresh lemon juice and simple syrup or honey (if you want a sweeter slush). Stir until the sweetener is dissolved.
2. Add the frozen mixed fruit (such as berries, peaches, or pineapple) to the wine mixture. Blend the entire mixture to make it liquid.
3. Pour the liquid mixture into the Ninja slushi vessel. Make sure not to overfill the machine.
4. Turn on the machine, select the SPIKED SLUSH setting to process the mixture.
5. Once the machine beeps three times, indicating the slushie is ready, carefully pour it into glasses.

### Nutrients (Per Serving):

Calories: ~150 | Carbohydrates: 15g | Sugar: 10g (mostly from the wine and fruit) | Protein: 0g | Fat: 0g | Fiber: 1g.

Gin and Tonic Slush

*Ingredients*:

- 1 cup gin (your preferred brand)
- ½ cup fresh lime juice (about 3-4 limes)
- 1 cup tonic water
- 1 tablespoon simple syrup or agave nectar (optional, for sweetness)
- Lime slices or wedges for garnish

**Prep**: 5 minutes

**Servings**: 2

*Instructions*:

1. In a large pitcher or bowl, mix the gin, fresh lime juice, tonic water, and simple syrup (if using).

2. Refrigerate the gin and tonic mixture for 10-15 minutes before processing
3. Pour the chilled mixture into the Ninja slushi vessel. Turn on the machine and select the SPIKED SLUSH preset to process the mixture.
4. The machine will beep three times when it's ready. Pour the slushie into glasses to enjoy!

*Nutrients (Approximate Per Serving):*

Calories: ~150 | Carbohydrates: 6g | Sugar: 5g | Protein: 0g | Fat: 0g | Fiber: 0g

## Low Sugar Strawberry Margarita

*Ingredients*:

- 2 cups frozen strawberries
- 1 cup tequila (silver or preferred type)
- ½ cup fresh lime juice (about 4 limes)
- ¼ cup orange liqueur (such as triple sec or Cointreau)
- 1 tablespoon agave syrup or stevia (optional, for sweetness)
- Salt for rimming glasses (optional)

**Prep:** 5 minutes

**Servings**: 2

*Instructions*:

1. If you prefer a salted rim, rub a lime wedge around the rim of each glass and dip it into salt.
2. In a pitcher or large bowl, combine the frozen strawberries, tequila, lime juice, orange liqueur, and agav syrup (or sweetener of choice).
3. In a blender, blend the mixture until smooth.

4. Let the blended mixture sit in the fridge for about 10-15 minutes to chill.
5. Pour the chilled mixture into the Ninja slushi vessel and select the SPIKED SLUSH preset to process the mixture.
6. Once the slushie is ready (the machine will beep three times), pour it into your prepared glasses.

### Nutrients (Per Serving) (Approximate):

Calories: ~120 | Carbohydrates: 8g | Sugar: 6g | Protein: 1g | Fat: 0g | Fiber: 3g.

Berry Sangria Slush

### Ingredients:

- 1 cup red wine (such as Merlot or Cabernet Sauvignon)
- ½ cup orange liqueur (such as Cointreau or Triple Sec)
- ½ cup fresh orange juice
- ½ cup fresh lemon juice
- ¼ cup simple syrup (optional, for added sweetness)
- ½ cup mixed frozen berries (strawberries, blueberries, raspberries)
- ½ cup frozen sliced peaches (optional)
- ½ cup club soda or sparkling water (for fizz)

**Prep**: 10 minutes

**Servings**: 2

### Instructions

1. In a large pitcher or bowl, mix together the red wine, orange liqueur, orange juice, lemon juice, and simple syrup (if using). Stir to combine.

2. Add the mixed frozen berries and optional frozen peaches to the pitcher with the liquid mix.

3. Blend the mixture until smooth. Let the mixture chill in the refrigerator for about 10-15 minutes.

4. Pour the chilled mixture into the Ninja slushi vessel and select the SPIKED SLUSH preset to process the mixture.

5. The machine will beep three times when it's ready. Once the slush is ready, gently stir in the club soda or sparkling water for a little fizz and added refreshment.

*Nutrients (Per Serving)*

Calories: ~170 I Carbohydrates: 22g I Sugar: 17g I Protein: 0g I Fat: 0g I Fiber: 3g

## Espresso Martini Slushie

*Ingredients:*

- 1 cup cold brewed espresso (or strong coffee)
- ½ cup vodka (your preferred brand)
- ¼ cup coffee liqueur (such as Kahlúa)
- 1 tablespoon simple syrup (optional, for sweetness)
- Garnish: Coffee beans or cocoa powder (optional)

**Prep**: 5 minutes

**Servings**: 2

*Instructions*

1. If you don't have cold brewed espresso, brew strong coffee and allow it to cool to room temperature. You can also chill it in the refrigerator.

2. In a cocktail shaker or mixing glass, combine the cold brewed espresso, vodka, coffee liqueur, and simple syrup (if desired). Stir well to combine the ingredients.
3. Pour the chilled mixture into the Ninja slushi vessel and select the SPIKED SLUSH preset to process the mixture.
4. The machine will beep three times when the slushie is ready. Dispense into glass and garnish with a few coffee beans or a sprinkle of cocoa powder for an extra touch.

### Nutrients (Approximate per Serving)

Calories: ~150-180 (depending on the amount of simple syrup used) | Carbohydrates: 15g | Sugar: 12g | Protein: 1g | Fat: 0g | Fiber: 0g

**Tips**: For an extra creamy touch, you can add a splash of cream or milk before blending.

## Rum and Coke Slush

### Ingredients:

- 1 cup dark rum (or your preferred rum)
- 2 cups Coca-Cola (or diet Coca-Cola, if preferred)
- 1 tablespoon fresh lime juice (optional, for added tang)
- 1-2 tablespoons simple syrup or agave nectar (optional, for added sweetness)

**Prep**: 5 minutes

**Servings**: 2-3

**Instructions**:

1. Pour the dark rum into a pitcher or large bowl. Add the Coca-Cola (or diet Coke) to the pitcher. You can also add the fresh lime juice and simple syrup if you prefer a tangier or sweeter flavor.
2. Chill the mixture in the fridge for 10-15 minutes

3. Pour the chilled mixture into the Ninja slushi vessel and select the SPIKED SLUSH preset to process the mixture.
4. The machine will beep three times once the slush is ready.

### Nutrients (Approximate per Serving)

Calories: ~200 | Carbohydrates: 20g | Sugar: 18g | Protein: 0g | Fat: 0g | Fiber: 0g

Cinnamon Whiskey Cider

### Ingredients:

- 1 cup cinnamon whiskey (e.g., Fireball)
- 1 cup apple cider
- ½ teaspoon ground cinnamon
- 1 tablespoon honey or simple syrup (optional, for added sweetness)

**Prep**: 5 minutes

**Servings**: 2

### Instructions:

1. In a mixing bowl or pitcher, combine the cinnamon whiskey, apple cider, ground cinnamon, and honey or simple syrup if you want extra sweetness.
2. Refrigerate the combined mixture for about 10-15 minutes.
3. Pour the chilled mixture into the Ninja slushi vessel and select the SPIKED SLUSH preset to process the mixture.
4. The machine will beep three times when the slush is ready.
5. Once the slush is ready, pour into glasses and garnish with a cinnamon stick or an apple slice.

*Nutrients (Per Serving) (Approximate):*

Calories: ~180 | Carbohydrates: 22g | Sugar: 18g | Protein: 0g | Fat: 0g | Fiber: 0g

## Mai Tai Slush

*Ingredients*:

- 1 cup light rum
- ½ cup dark rum
- ¼ cup lime juice (freshly squeezed)
- ¼ cup orange curaçao or orange liqueur
- 1 tablespoon orgeat syrup (almond-flavored syrup)
- ½ cup pineapple juice
- 1 tablespoon simple syrup or agave nectar (optional, for sweetness)

**Prep**: 5 minutes

**Servings**: 2-3

*Instructions*:

1. In a pitcher, combine the light rum, dark rum, lime juice, orange curaçao, orgeat syrup, and pineapple juice. Stir to combine the ingredients well. For extra sweetness, you can add the simple syrup or agave nectar to taste.
2. Refrigerate the combined mixture for about 10-15 minutes to cool it down.
3. Pour the chilled mixture into the Ninja slushi vessel and select the SPIKED SLUSH preset to process the mixture.
4. The machine will beep three times when the slush is ready.

### Nutrients (Per Serving):

Calories: ~180-200 (depending on the brand of rum and mixers used)| Carbohydrates: 15g | Sugar: 12g | Protein: 0g | Fat: 0g | Fiber: 0g

### Ingredients:

- 1 cup Aperol
- ½ cup Prosecco (or other sparkling wine)
- ½ cup club soda or sparkling water
- ½ cup fresh orange juice
- 1 tablespoon simple syrup or agave nectar (optional, for added sweetness)

**Prep:** 5 minutes

**Servings**: 2

### Instructions:

1. In a pitcher, mix the Aperol, Prosecco, club soda (or sparkling water), and fresh orange juice. If desired, add the simple syrup or agave nectar for a bit of extra sweetness. Stir well to combine.
2. Refrigerate the combined mixture for about 10-15 minutes.
3. Pour the chilled mixture into the Ninja slushi vessel and select the SPIKED SLUSH preset to process the mixture.
4. The machine will beep three times when it's ready.

### Nutrients (Per Serving) (Approximate):

Calories: ~150 | Carbohydrates: 8g | Sugar: 5g | Protein: 0g | Fat: 0g | Fiber: 0g

# Boozy Banana Split Slush

## Ingredients

- 1 medium ripe banana, sliced and frozen
- 1 cup milk (dairy or non-dairy)
- 2 tablespoons chocolate syrup
- 1 tablespoon caramel sauce
- 1 scoop vanilla ice cream
- 1 ounce rum (or substitute with ½ teaspoon vanilla extract for a non-alcoholic version)
- Whipped cream (optional, for garnish)
- Maraschino cherry (optional, for garnish)
- Crushed nuts or sprinkles (optional, for garnish)

**Prep**: 5 minutes

**Servings**: 1

## Instructions

1. In a blender, combine the frozen banana slices, milk, chocolate syrup, caramel sauce, vanilla ice cream, and rum. Blend until smooth.
2. Although optional, you can refrigerate the mixture for 5-10 minutes for extra coolness.
3. Pour the chilled mixture into the Ninja slushi vessel and select the FRAPPE preset to process the mixture.
4. Once the slushie is ready (indicated by the machine's triple beep), pour it into a tall glass.
5. Top with whipped cream, a drizzle of chocolate syrup, a maraschino cherry, and crushed nuts or sprinkles.

## Nutrients (Per Serving)

Calories: ~290 | Carbohydrates: 50g | Sugar: 35g | Protein: 4g | Fat: 7g | Fiber: 2g

# FRAPPES

56. Pumpkin Spice Slushie

57. Sugar Free Coffee Slushie

58. Mocha Frappe Slushie

59. Oatmeal Cookie Slushie

60. Hazelnut Frappe Slushie

61. White Chocolate Frappe Slushie

62. Mint Chocolate Frappe Slush

63. Peanut Butter Frappe Slush

64. Coconut Frappe Slushie

65. Tiramisu Frappe Slushie

66. Almond Joy Frappe Slush

67. Chai Tea Frappe Slush

68. Matcha Green Tea Frappe Slush

69. Caramel Frappe Slushie

70. Strawberry Cheesecake Slushie

71. Oreo Frappe Slush

72. Banana Mocha Slushie

73. Espresso Brownie Slush

# Pumpkin Spice Slushie

*Ingredients*:

- 1 cup brewed coffee (cooled)
- ½ cup milk (any kind—dairy, almond, oat, etc.)
- ½ cup canned pumpkin puree
- 2 tablespoons maple syrup or sweetener of choice (optional, for added sweetness)
- 1 teaspoon pumpkin spice (or to taste)
- Whipped cream for garnish (optional)
- Ground cinnamon for garnish (optional)

**Prep**: 5 minutes

**Servings**: 2

*Instructions:*

1. Brew the coffee and allow it to cool to room temperature or put it on the refrigerator.
2. In a blender, combine the cooled coffee, milk, pumpkin puree, maple syrup (or preferred sweetener), and pumpkin spice. Blend until smooth and well mixed.
3. Chill the mixture in the refrigerator for about 10–15 minutes, or you can skip this step if you prefer your frappe less icy.
4. Pour the chilled mixture into the Ninja slushi vessel and select the FRAPPE preset to process the mixture.
5. Once the slush is ready, the machine will beep three times, pour into glasses.
6. Garnish with whipped cream and a sprinkle of cinnamon on top.

*Nutrients (Per Serving) (Approximate):*

Calories: ~150 | Carbohydrates: 25g | Sugar: 22g | Protein: 2g | Fat: 4g | Fiber: 2g.

# Sugar Free Coffee Slushie

*Ingredients*:

- 1 cup brewed coffee (cooled to room temperature or chilled)
- ½ cup unsweetened almond milk (or any milk of your choice)
- 1 tablespoon sugar-free vanilla syrup (or your preferred sugar-free sweetener)
- Optional: Whipped cream (sugar-free) for topping

**Prep:** 5 minutes

**Servings**: 2

*Instructions:*

1. Brew 1 cup of coffee and allow it to cool to room temperature or chill it in the refrigerator for faster preparation.
2. In a pitcher, combine the cooled coffee, unsweetened almond milk, and sugar-free vanilla syrup.
3. Chill the mixture in the refrigerator for about 10–15 minutes.
4. Pour the chilled mixture into the Ninja slushi vessel and select the FRAPPE preset to process the mixture.
5. Once the slush is ready (the machine will beep three times), pour it into glasses.
6. Top with a dollop of sugar-free whipped cream for a creamier finish.

*Nutrients (Per Serving) (Approximate):*

Calories: ~20 (depending on milk and sweetener used) | Carbohydrates: 2g | Sugar: 0g | Protein: 1g | Fat: 1g (from almond milk, if used) | Fiber: 1g (from almond milk)

# Mocha Frappe Slushie

## Ingredients

- 1 cup strong brewed coffee, chilled
- ½ cup milk (dairy or non-dairy, as preferred)
- 2 tablespoons chocolate syrup
- 1 tablespoon sugar (optional, adjust to taste)
- ½ teaspoon vanilla extract

**Prep:** 5 minutes

**Servings:** 2

## Instructions

1. Brew a cup of strong coffee and let it cool completely. Preferably, chill it in the refrigerator or use pre-made iced coffee.
2. In a bowl, combine the chilled coffee, milk, chocolate syrup, sugar (if desired), and vanilla extract.
3. Place the mocha mixture in the refrigerator for 10–15 minutes.
4. Pour the chilled mixture into the Ninja slushi vessel and select the FRAPPE preset to process the mixture.
5. Once the slush is ready (the machine will beep three times), pour it into serving glasses.
6. Garnish with whipped cream, a drizzle of chocolate syrup, and a sprinkle of cocoa powder, if desired.

## Nutrients (Per Serving)

Calories: ~120 | Carbohydrates: 18g | Sugar: 15g | Protein: 3g | Fat: 2g | Fiber: 0g

# Oatmeal Cookie Slushie

## *Ingredients*

- 1 cup brewed and chilled coffee
- ½ cup oat milk
- ¼ cup rolled oats
- 2 tablespoons brown sugar
- ½ teaspoon ground cinnamon
- ½ teaspoon vanilla extract
- 1 tablespoon chocolate chips (optional, for garnish)

**Prep:** 10 minutes

**Servings:** 2

## *Instructions*

1. Brew your favorite coffee and allow it to chill in the refrigerator for at least 15 minutes.
2. In a blender, combine the chilled coffee, oat milk, rolled oats, brown sugar, cinnamon, and vanilla extract. Blend until smooth.
3. Transfer the blended mixture to the refrigerator and let it chill for about 5 minutes to enhance the texture.
4. Pour the chilled mixture into the Ninja slushi vessel and select the FRAPPE preset to process the mixture.
5. Once the slushie is ready (the machine will beep three times), pour it into glasses. Garnish with chocolate chips or a sprinkle of cinnamon.

## *Nutrients (Per Serving)*

Calories: ~120 | Carbohydrates: 22g | Sugar: 10g | Protein: 2g | Fat: 2g | Fiber: 2g

# Hazelnut Frappe Slushie

## *Ingredients*

- 1 cup strong brewed coffee (chilled)
- ½ cup milk (any type, dairy or non-dairy, as preferred)
- 3 tablespoons hazelnut syrup
- 1 tablespoon sugar or sweetener (optional, adjust based on sweetness level)
- Whipped cream (optional, for topping)
- Chopped hazelnuts or chocolate shavings (optional, for garnish)

**Prep:** 5 minutes

**Servings:** 2

## *Instructions*

1. Brew a strong cup of coffee and let it chill in the refrigerator. Use decaf if you prefer a caffeine-free option.
2. In a bowl, combine the chilled coffee, milk, hazelnut syrup, and sugar (if desired).
3. Refrigerate the mixture for about 10-15 minutes.
4. Pour the chilled mixture into the Ninja slushi vessel and select the FRAPPE preset to process the mixture.
5. Once the slushie is ready (indicated by the machine's triple beep), dispense the slush into two glasses.
6. Top with whipped cream, if desired, and garnish with chopped hazelnuts or chocolate shavings.

## *Nutrients (Per Serving)*

Calories: ~150 (varies based on milk type and additional toppings) | Carbohydrates: 22g | Sugar: 18g | Protein: 3g | Fat: 3g | Fiber: 0g

# White Chocolate Frappe Slushie

## *Ingredients*

- 1 cup cold milk (whole, almond, or oat milk works best)
- 2 tablespoons white chocolate chips or white chocolate syrup
- 1 shot of espresso or ¼ cup strong brewed coffee (optional for caffeine)
- Whipped cream (optional, for topping)
- White chocolate shavings or sprinkles (optional, for garnish)

**Prep:** 5 minutes

**Servings:** 1–2

## *Instructions*

1. If using white chocolate chips, gently melt them in a microwave-safe bowl. Let the melted chocolate cool slightly. If using white chocolate syrup, skip this step.
2. In a pitcher, combine the cold milk, melted white chocolate or syrup, and espresso or coffee (if using).
3. Refrigerate the mixture for about 10-15 minutes.
4. Pour the chilled mixture into the Ninja slushi vessel and select the FRAPPE preset to process the mixture.
5. The machine will beep three times when the slushie is ready, dispense the slushie into glasses.
6. Top with whipped cream, and garnish with white chocolate shavings or sprinkles.

## *Nutrients (Per Serving)*

Calories: ~200 | Carbohydrates: 26g | Sugar: 22g | Protein: 5g | Fat: 7g | Fiber: 0g

# Mint Chocolate Frappe Slush

## *Ingredients*

- 1 cup whole milk (or dairy-free alternative)
- ½ cup heavy cream (or coconut cream for non-dairy)
- ¼ cup mint chocolate syrup (or 2 tablespoons chocolate syrup + ¼ teaspoon peppermint extract)
- ¼ cup mini chocolate chips
- 1 tablespoon sugar (optional, depending on sweetness preference)
- Whipped cream (optional, for topping)
- Crushed mint candies or chocolate shavings (optional, for garnish)

**Prep:** 5 minutes

**Servings**: 2

## *Instructions*

1. In a blender, combine milk, heavy cream, mint chocolate syrup, sugar (if using), and mini chocolate chips. Blend until smooth and the ingredients are fully combined.
2. Place the mixture in the refrigerator for 5–10 minutes.
3. Pour the chilled mixture into the Ninja slushi vessel and select the FRAPPE preset to process the mixture.
4. Once the machine beeps three times to signal the slushie is ready, pour into glasses.
5. Top with whipped cream if desired and garnish with crushed mint candies, chocolate shavings, or additional mint chocolate syrup drizzle.

## *Nutrients (Per Serving) (Approximate)*

Calories: ~220 | Carbohydrates: 28g | Sugar: 22g | Protein: 5g | Fat: 10g| Fiber: 1g

# Peanut Butter Frappe Slush

## Ingredients:

- 1 cup milk (dairy or non-dairy, as preferred)
- 2 tablespoons creamy peanut butter
- 1 tablespoon chocolate syrup (optional, for extra flavor)
- 1 teaspoon vanilla extract
- 1 tablespoon honey or sweetener of choice (optional)

**Prep:** 10 minutes

**Servings**: 1–2

## Instructions:

1. In a pitcher, combine the milk, peanut butter, vanilla extract, chocolate syrup, and honey.
2. For best results, refrigerate the mixture for 10–15 minutes.
3. Pour the chilled mixture into the Ninja slushi vessel and select the FRAPPE preset to process the mixture
4. Once the machine beeps three times, indicating the frappe slush is ready, pour it into a tall glass.

## Nutrients (Per Serving):

Calories: ~200 | Carbohydrates: 15g | Sugar: 10g | Protein: 7g | Fat: 11g | Fiber: 1g

# Coconut Frappe Slushie

*Ingredients:*

- 1 cup unsweetened coconut milk
- ½ cup brewed coffee (cooled)
- 2 tablespoons coconut cream
- 2 tablespoons sugar or sweetener of choice (optional)
- 1 teaspoon vanilla extract

**Prep:** 5 minutes

**Servings**: 2

*Instructions:*

1. Brew coffee and let it cool to room temperature or chill in the refrigerator. If you prefer a richer flavor, use espresso instead of regular coffee.
2. In a bowl, combine the coconut milk, cooled coffee, coconut cream, sugar (if desired), and vanilla extract. Blend until smooth.
3. Transfer the mixture to the refrigerator for 10 minutes to chill.
4. Pour the chilled mixture into the Ninja slushi vessel and select the FRAPPE preset to process the mixture.
5. Once the machine beeps three times, indicating the slush is ready, pour it into a tall glass.
6. Top with a dollop of whipped cream, a sprinkle of toasted coconut flakes, or a drizzle of chocolate syrup.

*Nutrients (Per Serving):*

Calories: ~120 | Carbohydrates: 8g | Sugar: 5g | Protein: 1g | Fat: 9g | Fiber: 1g

# Tiramisu Frappe Slushie

## *Ingredients*

- 1 cup brewed espresso or strong coffee (chilled)
- 1 cup whole milk (or milk alternative)
- 2 tablespoons mascarpone cheese
- 2 tablespoons cocoa powder (plus extra for garnish)
- 2 tablespoons sugar or sweetener of choice
- 1 tablespoon coffee liqueur (optional, for a spiked version)

**Prep:** 10 minutes

**Servings:** 2

## *Instructions*

1. Brew the espresso or strong coffee and let it cool completely or chill in the refrigerator. If using coffee liqueur, set it aside.
2. In a bowl, combine the chilled espresso, milk, mascarpone cheese, cocoa powder, sugar, and optional coffee liqueur.
3. Transfer the mixture to the refrigerator for 10 minutes to chill.
4. Pour the chilled mixture into the Ninja slushi vessel and select the FRAPPE preset to process the mixture.
5. Once the slush is ready, the machine will beep three times. Pour the slush into glasses and dust the top with a light layer of cocoa powder or shaved chocolate.
6. You can also garnish with a ladyfinger biscuit on the side.

## *Nutrients (Per Serving)*

Calories: ~200 | Carbohydrates: 25g | Sugar: 20g | Protein: 5g | Fat: 7g | Fiber: 2g

# Almond Joy Frappe Slush

*Ingredients:*

- 1 cup unsweetened almond milk
- 2 tablespoons chocolate syrup
- 1 tablespoon coconut cream
- 1 tablespoon almond butter
- 1 teaspoon vanilla extract
- 1 cup strong brewed coffee (chilled)

**Prep:** 10 minutes

**Servings:** 2

*Instructions*:

1. Brew a cup of strong coffee and allow it to cool completely. For faster cooling, place it in the refrigerator or freezer for a few minutes.
2. In a pitcher, combine the chilled coffee, almond milk, chocolate syrup, coconut cream, almond butter, and vanilla extract.
3. Chill the mixture in the refrigerator for 15–20 minutes.
4. Pour the chilled mixture into the Ninja slushi vessel and select the FRAPPE preset to process the mixture.
5. Once the machine beeps three times, indicating the slush is ready, pour it into a tall glass.
6. Garnish with a drizzle of chocolate syrup, a sprinkle of shredded coconut, and a few almond slices for extra flair.

*Nutrients (Per Serving):*

Calories: ~190 | Carbohydrates: 15g | Sugar: 10g | Protein: 4g | Fat: 10g | Fiber: 2g

# Chai Tea Frappe Slush

## *Ingredients*

- 1 cup brewed chai tea (strong, chilled)
- ½ cup milk (dairy or non-dairy)
- 2 tablespoons honey or maple syrup (optional, for added sweetness)
- ½ teaspoon ground cinnamon
- ½ teaspoon ground cardamom

**Prep:** 10 minutes

**Servings:** 2

## *Instructions*

1. Brew a strong cup of chai tea using a chai tea bag or loose-leaf tea. Allow it to cool completely, or preferably chill it in the refrigerator.
2. In a blender, combine the chilled chai tea, milk, honey or maple syrup (if desired), ground cinnamon, and ground cardamom. Blend until smooth and well mixed.
3. Place the blended chai mixture in the refrigerator for 10–15 minutes.
4. Pour the chilled mixture into the Ninja slushi vessel and select the FRAPPE preset to process the mixture
5. Once the machine beeps three times, indicating the slush is ready, pour it into glasses.
6. Garnish with a sprinkle of cinnamon or a cinnamon stick.

## *Nutrients (Per Serving)*

Calories: ~120 | Carbohydrates: 24g | Sugar: 18g | Protein: 3g | Fat: 2g | Fiber: 1g

# Matcha Green Tea Frappe Slush

## Ingredients

- 1 ½ teaspoons matcha green tea powder
- 1 cup milk (dairy or plant-based, as preferred)
- 2 tablespoons granulated sugar or honey (adjust to taste)
- ½ teaspoon vanilla extract
- Whipped cream for garnish (optional)

**Prep:** 5 minutes

**Servings**: 2

## Instructions

1. In a small bowl, sift the matcha green tea powder to remove any clumps. Add a few tablespoons of warm (not boiling) milk to the matcha and whisk vigorously until it forms a smooth paste.
2. In a bowl, combine the matcha paste, remaining milk, sugar (or honey), and vanilla extract.
3. Chill the mixture in the refrigerator for 10–15 minutes.
4. Pour the chilled mixture into the Ninja slushi vessel and select the FRAPPE preset to process the mixture.
5. Once the machine finishes (it will beep three times), dispense the slush into glasses.
6. Garnish with whipped cream and a sprinkle of matcha powder, if desired.

## *Nutrients (Per Serving)*

Calories: ~120 I Carbohydrates: 22g I Protein: 4g I Fat: 2g I Fiber: 0g

# Caramel Frappe Slushie

### *Ingredients*:

- 1 cup strong brewed coffee, chilled
- ½ cup milk (dairy or non-dairy, as preferred)
- 2 tablespoons caramel sauce, plus extra for garnish
- Whipped cream (optional, for topping)

**Prep:** 10 minutes

**Servings**: 2

### *Instructions*:

1. Brew strong coffee and let it cool completely or chill the coffee in the refrigerator.
2. In a bowl, combine the chilled coffee, milk, and caramel sauce.
3. Place the mixture in the refrigerator for 10-15 minutes.
4. Pour the chilled mixture into the Ninja slushi vessel and select the FRAPPE preset to process the mixture.
5. Once the machine finishes (it will beep three times), dispense the slush into glasses.
6. Top with whipped cream if desired and drizzle extra caramel sauce over the top for garnish.

### *Nutrients (Per Serving):*

Calories: ~120 (without whipped cream) | Carbohydrates: 20g | Sugar: 18g | Protein: 3g | Fat: 3g

# Strawberry Cheesecake Slushie

*Ingredients*:

- 1 cup frozen strawberries
- ½ cup cream cheese, softened
- 1 cup cold milk (dairy or non-dairy)
- 2 tablespoons graham cracker crumbs (plus extra for garnish)
- 2 tablespoons sugar or sweetener (adjust to taste)
- ½ teaspoon vanilla extract

**Prep:** 10 minutes

**Servings**: 2

*Instructions*:

1. Soften the cream cheese slightly by leaving it at room temperature for about 5 minutes.
2. In a blender, combine the frozen strawberries, softened cream cheese, milk, graham cracker crumbs, sugar, and vanilla extract. Blend until the mixture is smooth.
3. To enhance the slush texture, chill the blended mixture in the refrigerator for 10 minutes.
4. Pour the chilled mixture into the Ninja slushi vessel and select the FRAPPE preset to process the mixture.
5. Once the machine finishes (it will beep three times), dispense the slush into glasses.
6. Top with a sprinkle of graham cracker crumbs for a classic cheesecake touch. Add a fresh strawberry or a dollop of whipped cream for extra flair.

*Nutrients (Per Serving):*

Calories: ~250 | Carbohydrates: 28g |Sugar: 22g | Protein: 5g | Fat: 10g | Fiber: 2g

## Ingredients:

- 2 cups vanilla ice cream
- 1 cup milk (whole or your preferred variety)
- 4 Oreo cookies (broken into pieces)
- 1 tablespoon chocolate syrup (optional)
- Whipped cream (for topping, optional)

**Prep**: 5 minutes

**Servings**: 2

## Instructions:

1. In a blender, combine the vanilla ice cream, milk, Oreo cookies, and chocolate syrup (if using). Blend until the mixture is smooth
2. Chill the blended mixture in the refrigerator for 10 minutes.
3. Pour the chilled mixture into the Ninja slushi vessel and select the FRAPPE preset to process the mixture
4. Once the machine finishes (it will beep three times), dispense the slush into glasses.
5. Top with whipped cream and additional crushed Oreos or chocolate syrup

## Nutrients (Per Serving) (Approximate):

Calories: ~250 | Carbohydrates: 32g | Sugar: 23g | Protein: 4g | Fat: 12g | Fiber: 1g

# Banana Mocha Slushie

## Ingredients

- 1 medium ripe banana, sliced and frozen
- 1 cup brewed coffee, chilled
- ½ cup milk (dairy or non-dairy, as preferred)
- 2 tablespoons cocoa powder
- 1–2 tablespoons sugar or sweetener (optional, to taste)
- Whipped cream and chocolate shavings (optional, for garnish)

**Prep:** 10 minutes

**Servings:** 2

## Instructions

1. In a blender, combine the frozen banana, chilled coffee, milk, cocoa powder, and sugar (if using). Blend until smooth.
2. Pour the mixture into the Ninja slushi vessel and select the FRAPPE preset to process the mixture.
3. Once the slush is ready (the machine will beep three times), pour it into glasses. Top with whipped cream and chocolate shavings if desired.

## Nutrients (Per Serving)

Calories: ~150 | Carbohydrates: 28g | Protein: 4g | Fat: 2g | Sugar: 20g | Fiber: 3g

# Espresso Brownie Slush

## *Ingredients*

- 1 cup brewed espresso, cooled
- ½ cup milk (whole, almond, or your preference)
- 2 tablespoons chocolate syrup
- 1 brownie, crumbled into small pieces (plus extra for garnish)
- 1 tablespoon sugar (optional, based on sweetness preference)
- Whipped cream (optional, for topping)

**Prep:** 5 minutes

**Servings:** 2

## *Instructions*

1. Brew the espresso and allow it to cool completely or chill it in the refrigerator.
2. In a blender, combine the espresso, milk, chocolate syrup, crumbled brownie, and sugar (if using). Blend until smooth.
3. Refrigerate the blended mixture for 5-10 minutes.
4. Pour the chilled mixture into the Ninja slushi vessel and select the FRAPPE preset to process the mixture.
5. Once the slush is ready (the machine will beep three times), pour it into glasses.
6. Top with whipped cream and sprinkle crumbled brownie pieces for garnish, if desired.

## *Nutrients (Per Serving)*

Calories: ~180 | Carbohydrates: 28g | Sugar: 22g | Protein: 3g | Fat: 6g | Fiber: 1g

**Tips:** For a stronger coffee flavor, use double shots of espresso.

# MILKSHAKES

74. Caramel Milkshake Slushie

75. S'mores Milkshake Slushie

76. Cinnamon Roll Milkshake Slush

77. Pistachio Milkshake Slushie

78. Hot Cocoa Milkshake Slushie

79. Blueberry Cheesecake Milkshake Slushie

80. Banana Nutella Milkshake Slush

81. Chocolate Milkshake Slushie

82. Creamsicle Milkshake Slushie

83. Vanilla Milkshake Slushie

84. Black Forest Milkshake Slush

85. Mango Lassi Milkshake Slush

86. Red Velvet Cake Milkshake Slushie

87. Cookies & Cream Milkshake Slush

88. Pumpkin Pie Milkshake Slush

89. Peach Cobbler Milkshake Slush

# Caramel Milkshake Slushie

## *Ingredients:*

- 2 cups vanilla ice cream
- 1 cup cold milk (whole milk or your preferred type)
- 3 tablespoons caramel sauce (plus extra for garnish)
- Whipped cream (optional, for topping)

**Prep:** 5 minutes

**Servings**: 2

## *Instructions*:

1. In a bowl, combine the vanilla ice cream, cold milk, and caramel sauce.
2. Chill the mixture in the freezer for 10–15 minutes.
3. Pour the mixture into the Ninja slushi vessel and select the MILKSHAKE preset to process the mixture
4. Once the slushie is ready (the machine will beep three times), pour it into glasses.
5. Garnish with a drizzle of caramel sauce along the inside of the glass or on top of the slushi.

## *Nutrients (Per Serving) (Approximate):*

Calories: ~300 | Carbohydrates: 42g | Sugar: 38g | Protein: 6g | Fat: 12g

**Tips**: Add a pinch of sea salt for a salted caramel twist.

# S'mores Milkshake Slushie

## Ingredients

- 2 cups vanilla ice cream
- 1 cup whole milk (or milk alternative of choice)
- 3 tablespoons chocolate syrup
- 4 graham crackers (divided, 2 for blending and 2 for garnish)
- ¼ cup mini marshmallows
- 1 tablespoon toasted marshmallow topping (optional, for garnish)
- Whipped cream (optional, for garnish)

**Prep:** 5 minutes

**Servings**: 2

## Instructions

1. Toast marshmallows (optional) using a kitchen torch or broiler for added flavor.
2. In a blender, combine the vanilla ice cream, milk, chocolate syrup, graham cracker pieces, and mini marshmallows. Blend until smooth and creamy.
3. Place the blended milkshake mixture in the refrigerator for about 10–15 minutes.
4. Pour the mixture into the Ninja slushi vessel and select the MILKSHAKE preset to process the mixture
5. Once the slushie is ready (the machine will beep three times), pour it into glasses.
6. Top with whipped cream, toasted marshmallow topping, and crushed graham crackers. Drizzle additional chocolate syrup if desired.

## Nutrients (Per Serving)

Calories: ~300 | Carbohydrates: 50g | Sugar: 36g | Protein: 6g | Fat: 10g | Fiber: 1g.

# Cinnamon Roll Milkshake Slush

## Ingredients:

- 2 cups vanilla ice cream
- 1 cup milk (whole or any milk of choice)
- 1 teaspoon ground cinnamon
- 1 teaspoon vanilla extract
- 1 tablespoon brown sugar (optional, for added sweetness)
- 1 cinnamon roll (store-bought or homemade), cut into small pieces
- Whipped cream and cinnamon powder for garnish

**Prep**: 10 minutes

**Servings**: 2

## Instructions:

1. In a blender, combine the vanilla ice cream, milk, ground cinnamon, vanilla extract, brown sugar (if using), and cinnamon roll pieces. Blend until smooth and creamy.
2. Place the blended milkshake in the refrigerator for 10-15 minutes.
3. Pour the mixture into the Ninja slushi vessel and select the MILKSHAKE preset to process the mixture
4. Once the slushie is ready (the machine will beep three times), pour it into tall glasses.
5. Top with a generous dollop of whipped cream and a sprinkle of cinnamon powder for garnish.

## Nutrients (Per Serving):

Calories: ~320 | Carbohydrates: 45g | Sugar: 35g | Protein: 6g | Fat: 12g | Fiber: 1g

# Pistachio Milkshake Slushie

*Ingredients*:

- 2 cups vanilla ice cream
- 1 ½ cups whole milk (cold)
- ½ cup shelled pistachios (unsalted)
- 2 tablespoons honey or sugar (optional, adjust to taste)
- Whipped cream and chopped pistachios (for garnish, optional)

**Prep**: 10 minutes

**Servings**: 2

*Instructions*:

1. Place the pistachios in a food processor or blender and pulse until finely ground. If desired, reserve a small amount of the chopped pistachios for garnish.
2. Add the vanilla ice cream, cold whole milk, and honey or sugar (if desired) to the blender. Blend until smooth and creamy.
3. Transfer the blended pistachio milkshake to the refrigerator for 5–10 minutes.
4. Pour the mixture into the Ninja slushi vessel and select the MILKSHAKE preset to process the mixture
5. Once the slushie is ready (the machine will beep three times), pour it into serving glasses.
6. Top with whipped cream and sprinkle with the reserved chopped pistachios.

*Nutrients (Per Serving)*:

Calories: ~320 | Carbohydrates: 36g | Sugar: 28g | Protein: 7g | Fat: 16g | Fiber: 2g

# Hot Cocoa Milkshake Slushie

## *Ingredients:*

- 2 cups whole milk (or your preferred milk)
- ½ cup hot cocoa mix (choose your favorite brand or homemade)
- 2 tablespoons sugar (optional, for extra sweetness)
- ½ cup chocolate ice cream
- ½ cup vanilla ice cream
- Whipped cream (for topping, optional)
- Chocolate shavings or cocoa powder (for garnish, optional)

**Prep**: 5 minutes

**Servings**: 2

## *Instructions*:

1. In a medium bowl, combine the whole milk and hot cocoa mix. Stir well until the cocoa mix is fully dissolved. Add the sugar (if desired), and stir until it is fully incorporated.
2. Place the chocolate and vanilla ice cream in the blender, then add the milk and hot cocoa mixture. Blend until smooth and creamy.
3. Transfer the blended mixture to the refrigerator for 10–15 minutes.
4. Pour the chilled mixture into the Ninja slushi vessel and select the MILKSHAKE preset to process the mixture
5. Once the slushie is ready (the machine will beep three times), pour it into serving glasses.
6. Top with whipped cream, chocolate shavings, or a sprinkle of cocoa powder.

## *Nutrients (Per Serving)*:

Calories: ~250 | Carbohydrates: 30g | Sugar: 22g | Protein: 6g | Fat: 12g | Fiber: 1g

# Blueberry Cheesecake Milkshake Slushie

*Ingredients*:

- 1 cup fresh or frozen blueberries
- 1 cup vanilla ice cream
- ½ cup milk (dairy or non-dairy)
- 2 tablespoons cream cheese (softened)
- 1 tablespoon honey or sugar (optional, for added sweetness)
- 1 teaspoon vanilla extract

**Prep:** 5 minutes

**Servings**: 2

*Instructions*:

1. In a blender, combine the blueberries, vanilla ice cream, milk, cream cheese, and vanilla extract. Blend until smooth.
2. Place the blended mixture in the refrigerator for 10-15 minutes to chill.
3. Pour the chilled mixture into the Ninja slushi vessel and select the MILKSHAKE preset to process the mixture
4. Once the slushie is ready (the machine will beep three times), pour it into serving glasses.

*Nutrients (Per Serving) (Approximate):*

Calories: ~250 | Carbohydrates: 32g | Sugar: 28g | Protein: 5g | Fat: 12g | Fiber: 3g

# Banana Nutella Milkshake Slush

### Ingredients:

- 2 ripe bananas (peeled and sliced)
- 2 tablespoons Nutella (or any chocolate hazelnut spread)
- 1 cup milk (whole milk or your preferred choice, such as almond or oat milk)
- 1 teaspoon vanilla extract (optional, for extra flavor)
- Whipped cream (optional, for topping)

**Prep:** 5 minutes

**Servings**: 2

### Instructions:

1. Peel and slice the bananas into smaller chunks to make blending easier.
2. In a blender, combine the sliced bananas, Nutella, milk, and vanilla extract (if using). Blend until the mixture is smooth and creamy.
3. Place the mixture in the fridge for 10–15 minutes.
4. Pour the chilled mixture into the Ninja slushi vessel and select the MILKSHAKE preset to process the mixture
5. Once the slushie is ready (the machine will beep three times), pour it into serving glasses.
6. Optionally, top with whipped cream for an indulgent touch.

### Nutrients (Per Serving) (Approximate):

Calories: ~250| Carbohydrates: 35g | Sugar: 28g | Protein: 4g | Fat: 11g | Fiber: 3g

# Chocolate Milkshake Slushie

*Ingredients*:

- 2 cups vanilla ice cream (or chocolate, if preferred)
- 1 cup milk (whole or your preferred type)
- ¼ cup chocolate syrup (or to taste)
- ½ teaspoon vanilla extract (optional)
- Whipped cream for topping (optional)
- Chocolate shavings or sprinkles (optional for garnish)

**Prep:** 5 minutes

**Servings**: 2

*Instructions*:

1. In a pitcher, combine the vanilla ice cream, milk, chocolate syrup, and vanilla extract (if using).
2. Place the mixture in the refrigerator to chill for about 15 minutes.
3. Pour the chilled mixture into the Ninja slushi vessel and select the MILKSHAKE preset to process the mixture
4. Once the slushie is ready (the machine will beep three times), pour it into serving glasses.
5. Top with whipped cream, chocolate shavings, or sprinkles for extra flair.

*Nutrients (Per Serving):*

Calories: ~320 | Carbohydrates: 35g | Sugar: 30g | Protein: 4g | Fat: 16g | Fiber: 1g

# Creamsicle Milkshake Slushie

### Ingredients:

- 2 cups vanilla ice cream
- 1 cup orange juice (freshly squeezed for the best flavor)
- ½ cup milk (or dairy-free alternative)
- 1 tablespoon honey or sweetener (optional, depending on desired sweetness)
- 1 teaspoon vanilla extract (optional, for extra flavor)

**Prep:** 5 minutes

**Servings:** 2

### Instructions:

1. In a pitcher, combine the vanilla ice cream, orange juice, milk, honey (or sweetener), and vanilla extract.
2. Transfer the mixture to the refrigerator for about 10-15 minutes.
3. Pour the chilled mixture into the Ninja slushi vessel and select the MILKSHAKE preset to process the mixture
4. Once the slushie is ready (the machine will beep three times), pour it into serving glasses.

### Nutrients (Per Serving) (Approximate):

Calories: ~250 | Carbohydrates: 35g | Sugar: 28g | Protein: 4g | Fat: 8g | Fiber: 0g

# Vanilla Milkshake Slushie

*Ingredients*:

- 2 cups vanilla ice cream
- 1 cup milk (whole or your preferred variety)
- 1 tablespoon vanilla extract
- 1 tablespoon sugar (optional, depending on desired sweetness)
- Whipped cream for topping (optional)
- Maraschino cherry for garnish (optional)

**Prep:** 5 minutes

**Servings**: 2

*Instructions*:

1. In a bowl, mix vanilla ice cream, milk, vanilla extract, and sugar (if using).
2. Chill the mixture in the refrigerator for about 10-15 minutes.
3. Pour the chilled mixture into the Ninja slushi vessel and select the MILKSHAKE preset to process the mixture
4. Once the slushie is ready (the machine will beep three times), pour it into serving glasses.
5. Top with whipped cream and a maraschino cherry if desired.

*Nutrients (Per Serving) (Approximate):*

Calories: ~300 | Carbohydrates: 35g | Sugar: 28g | Protein: 6g | Fat: 15g | Fiber: 0g

# Black Forest Milkshake Slush

*Ingredients*:

- 2 cups vanilla ice cream
- 1 cup milk (dairy or non-dairy)
- ½ cup chocolate syrup
- ½ cup canned cherry pie filling (or fresh cherries)
- Whipped cream (for topping)
- Maraschino cherries (for garnish)

**Prep:** 5 minutes

**Servings**: 2

*Instructions*:

1. In a blender, combine the vanilla ice cream, milk, chocolate syrup, and cherry pie filling. Blend until smooth.
2. Chill the blended mixture in the refrigerator for about 10 minutes.
3. Pour the chilled mixture into the Ninja slushi vessel and select the MILKSHAKE preset to process the mixture
4. Once the slushie is ready (the machine will beep three times), pour it into serving glasses.
5. Top with a swirl of whipped cream, drizzle some chocolate syrup, and garnish with maraschino cherries.

*Nutrients (Approximate per serving):*

Calories: ~380 | Carbohydrates: 50g | Sugar: 45g | Protein: 6g | Fat: 18g | Fiber: 1g

*Ingredients:*

- 2 cups fresh or frozen mango chunks
- 1 cup plain yogurt (preferably full-fat for creaminess)
- ½ cup milk (any type, dairy or non-dairy)
- 1 tablespoon honey or sugar (optional, depending on sweetness preference)
- ¼ teaspoon ground cardamom (optional, for authentic flavor)

**Prep**: 10 minutes

**Servings**: 2

*Instructions*:

1. In a blender, combine the mango chunks, yogurt, milk, honey or sugar, and cardamom (if using). Blend until smooth and creamy.
2. Chill the blended mixture in the refrigerator for about 10 minutes.
3. Pour the chilled mixture into the Ninja slushi vessel and select the MILKSHAKE preset to process the mixture
4. Once the slushie is ready (the machine will beep three times), pour it into serving glasses and garnish with a sprinkle of ground cardamom or a fresh mint leaf.

*Nutrients (Per Serving):*

Calories: ~180 | Carbohydrates: 35g | Sugar: 30g (may vary based on mango and sweetener) | Protein: 4g | Fat: 3g (from yogurt) | Fiber: 3g.

# Red Velvet Cake Milkshake Slushie

*Ingredients:*

- 1 cup vanilla ice cream
- ½ cup milk (whole or skim, your preference)
- ¼ cup red velvet cake mix (or 1 slice of red velvet cake, crumbled)
- 1 tablespoon cream cheese (optional, for added richness)
- ½ teaspoon vanilla extract
- ½ cup whipped cream (optional, for topping)
- 1 maraschino cherry (optional, for garnish)

**Prep:** 5 minutes

**Servings**: 2

*Instructions*:

1. If using a slice of red velvet cake, crumble it into smaller pieces. If you're using cake mix, it's already in powder form, so no prep is needed.
2. In a blender, combine the vanilla ice cream, milk, red velvet cake mix (or crumbled cake), cream cheese (if using), and vanilla extract. Blend until smooth and creamy.
3. Chill the blended mixture in the refrigerator for about 10 minutes.
4. Pour the chilled mixture into the Ninja slushi vessel and select the MILKSHAKE preset to process the mixture
5. Once the slushie is ready (the machine will beep three times), pour it into serving glasses.
6. Add a generous swirl of whipped cream and garnish with a maraschino cherry.

Nutrients (Approximate) (Per Serving):

Calories: ~300 | Carbohydrates: 45g | Sugar: 35g | Protein: 4g | Fat: 15g | Fiber: 1g

# Cookies & Cream Milkshake Slush

*Ingredients*:

- 2 cups vanilla ice cream
- 1 cup milk (whole, skim, or your preferred milk)
- 6-8 Oreo cookies (or other chocolate sandwich cookies)
- 1 tablespoon chocolate syrup (optional for extra richness)
- ½ teaspoon vanilla extract (optional for added flavor)

**Prep:** 5 minutes

**Servings**: 2

*Instructions*:

1. In a blender, combine the vanilla ice cream, milk, Oreo cookie pieces, and optional chocolate syrup or vanilla extract. Blend until smooth.
2. Refrigerate the mixture for about 10-15 minutes.
3. Pour the chilled mixture into the Ninja slushi vessel and select the MILKSHAKE preset to process the mixture
4. Once the slushie is ready (the machine will beep three times), pour it into serving glasses.
5. Optionally, you can top with whipped cream and more crushed Oreo cookies.

*Nutrients (Approximate, Per Serving):*

Calories: ~300 | Carbohydrates: 40g | Sugar: 35g | Protein: 5g | Fat: 15g| Fiber: 2g

# Pumpkin Pie Milkshake Slush

### Ingredients:

- 2 cups vanilla ice cream
- ½ cup canned pumpkin puree
- ½ cup milk (or more for desired consistency)
- ¼ cup brown sugar (or maple syrup for a lighter version)
- ½ teaspoon ground cinnamon
- ¼ teaspoon ground nutmeg
- ¼ teaspoon ground ginger
- ¼ teaspoon ground cloves (optional)
- Whipped cream for topping (optional)

**Prep:** 5 minutes

**Servings**: 2

### Instructions:

1. In a blender, combine the vanilla ice cream, pumpkin puree, milk, brown sugar, cinnamon, nutmeg, ginger, and cloves. Blend until smooth and well combined.
2. Place the mixture in the refrigerator for 10-15 minutes.
3. Pour the chilled mixture into the Ninja slushi vessel and select the MILKSHAKE preset to process the mixture
4. Once the slush is ready (the machine will beep three times), pour it into glasses.
5. Top with whipped cream, a sprinkle of cinnamon or nutmeg, or even a mini graham cracker crust rim.

### Nutrients (Per Serving) (Approximate):

Calories: ~300-350 | Carbohydrates: 45g | Sugar: 35g | Protein: 5g | Fat: 15g | Fiber: 2g

# Peach Cobbler Milkshake Slush

*Ingredients*:

- 2 cups frozen peach slices
- ½ cup vanilla ice cream
- ½ cup milk (or milk alternative)
- 1 tablespoon brown sugar
- 1 teaspoon cinnamon
- 1 teaspoon vanilla extract
- ¼ cup crumbled graham crackers (optional for texture)

**Prep:** 5 minutes

**Servings**: 2

*Instructions:*

1. In a blender, combine frozen peach slices, vanilla ice cream, milk, brown sugar, cinnamon, and vanilla extract. Blend until smooth and well combined.
2. If you want a colder slush, place the mixture in the freezer for about 10 minutes.
3. Pour the chilled mixture into the Ninja slushi vessel and select the MILKSHAKE preset to process the mixture
4. Once the slush is ready (the machine will beep three times), pour it into glasses and sprinkle some crumbled graham crackers on top.

*Nutrients (Per Serving) (Approximate):*

Calories: ~300 | Carbohydrates: 40g | Sugar: 32g | Protein: 5g | Fat: 10g | Fiber: 3g

# FROZEN JUICES

90. Watermelon Frozen Juice Slush

91. Pineapple Frozen Juice Slush

92. Cranberry Frozen Juice Slush

93. Pineapple Mango Frozen Juice Slush

94. Cranberry Raspberry Frozen Juice Slush

95. Cranberry Pomegranate Frozen Juice Slush

96. Grapefruit Frozen Juice Slush

97. Cranberry Mango Frozen Juice Slush

98. Mango Frozen Juice Slush

99. Berry Frozen Juice Slush

100. Orange Pineapple Frozen Juice Slush

101. Raspberry Frozen Juice Slush

102. Cherry Frozen Juice Slush

103. Apple Frozen Juice Slush

104. Tangerine Frozen Juice Slush

105. Lemonade Frozen Juice Slush

106. Peach Frozen Juice Slush

107. Dragon Fruit Frozen Juice Slush

# Watermelon Frozen Juice Slush

## Ingredients

- 2 cups of watermelon fruit drink (from any brand)
- 1-2 tablespoons of water (for adjusting thickness)

**Prep:** 5 minutes

**Servings**: 2

## Instructions

1. Put the watermelon fruit drink in the refrigerator for 10-15 minutes.
2. Pour the chilled drink into the Ninja slushi vessel and add the bit of water to help blend the mixture.
3. Turn on the machine, select the FROZEN JUICE preset, and let it process.
4. Once the slush is ready (the machine will beep three times), pour into glasses and serve immediately.

## Nutritional Value (per serving)

Calories: ~45 | Carbohydrates: 11g | Sugar: 9g | Protein: 0g | Fat: 0g | Fiber: 0g

# Pineapple Frozen Juice Slush

## Ingredients

- 2 cups of pineapple fruit drink (from any brand)
- 1 tablespoon honey (optional)

**Prep**: 5 minutes

**Servings**: 2

*Instructions*

1. Put the pineapple fruit drink in the refrigerator for 10-15 minutes.
2. Pour the chilled drink into the Ninja slushi vessel and add the teaspoon of honey for added sweetness.
3. Turn on the machine, select the FROZEN JUICE preset, and let it process.
4. Once the slush is ready (the machine will beep three times), pour into glasses and serve immediately.

*Nutritional Value (per serving)*

Calories: ~60 | Carbohydrates: 15g | Sugar: 12g | Protein: 0g | Fat: 0g | Fiber: 0g

Cranberry Frozen Juice Slush

*Ingredients*

- 2 cups of cranberry fruit drink (from any brand)
- 1-2 teaspoons honey or agave syrup (optional, for sweetness)

**Prep:** 5 minutes

**Servings**: 2

*Instructions*

1. Put the cranberry fruit drink in the refrigerator for 10-15 minutes
2. Pour the chilled drink into the Ninja Slushi machine's vessel. Add honey or agave syrup (if using).
3. Turn on the machine, select the FROZEN JUICE preset, and let it process.
4. Once the slush is ready (the machine will beep three times), pour into glasses and serve immediately.

*Nutritional Value (per serving)*

Calories: ~50 | Carbohydrates: 12g | Sugar: 10g | Protein: 0g | Fat: 0g | Fiber: 0g

Pineapple Mango Frozen Juice Slush

*Ingredients*

- 2 cups pineapple mango fruit drink (from any brand)

**Prep:** 5 minutes

**Servings**: 2

*Instructions*

1. Chill the pineapple mango drink in the refrigerator for 10–15 minutes.
2. Pour the chilled drink into the Ninja Slushi machine's vessel.
3. Turn on the machine, select the FROZEN JUICE preset, and let it process.
4. Once the slush is ready (indicated by three beeps), pour into glasses and serve immediately.

Calories: ~100 | Carbohydrates: ~25g | Sugar: ~22g | Protein: 0g | Fat: 0g

Cranberry Raspberry Frozen Juice Slush

### Ingredients

- 2 cups of cranberry raspberry fruit drink (any brand)
- 1–2 teaspoons honey or agave syrup (optional, for sweetness)

**Prep:** 5 minutes

**Servings:** 2

### Instructions

1. Chill the cranberry raspberry fruit drink in the refrigerator for 10–15 minutes.
2. Pour the chilled drink into the Ninja Slushi machine's vessel. Add honey or agave syrup, if desired.
3. Turn on the machine and select the FROZEN JUICE preset. Allow it to process.
4. Once the slushie is ready (three beeps), pour into glasses and serve immediately.

### Nutritional Value (per serving)

Calories: ~60 | Carbohydrates: 14g | Sugar: 12g | Protein: 0g | Fat: 0g | Fiber: 0g

## Ingredients

- 2 cup cranberry pomegranate fruit drink (any brand)
- 1-2 teaspoons honey or agave syrup (optional, for sweetness)

**Prep:** 5 minutes

**Servings**: 2

## Instructions

1. Chill the cranberry pomegranate fruit drinks in the refrigerator for 10–15 minutes.
2. Pour the chilled drink into the Ninja Slushi machine's vessel, and add honey or agave syrup, if desired.
3. Turn on the machine, select the FROZEN JUICE preset, and allow it to process.
4. Once the slush is ready (signaled by three beeps), pour into glasses to enjoy.

### Nutritional Value (per serving)

Calories: ~60 | Carbohydrates: 14g | Sugar: 12g | Protein: 0g | Fat: 0g | Fiber: 0g

# Grapefruit Frozen Juice Slush

## Ingredients

- 2 cups of grapefruit juice drink (any brand)
- 1–2 teaspoons honey or agave syrup (optional, for added sweetness)

**Prep**: 5 minutes

**Servings**: 2

*Instructions*

1. Chill the grapefruit juice drink in the refrigerator for 10–15 minutes.
2. Pour the chilled juice into the Ninja Slushi machine's vessel. Add honey or agave syrup, if desired.
3. Turn on the machine and select the FROZEN JUICE preset. Allow it to process until the slushie is ready (indicated by three beeps).
4. Pour into glasses and serve immediately.

*Nutritional Value (per serving)*

Calories: ~45 | Carbohydrates: 10g | Sugar: 9g | Protein: 0g | Fat: 0g | Fiber: 0g

Cranberry Mango Frozen Juice Slush

*Ingredients*:

- 2 cups of cranberry mango fruit drink (any brand)
- 1–2 teaspoons honey or agave syrup (optional, for sweetness)

**Prep:** 5 minutes

**Servings**: 2

*Instructions*

1. Chill the cranberry mango drink in the refrigerator for 10–15 minutes.
2. Pour the chilled juice in the Ninja Slushi machine's vessel. Add honey or agave syrup, if using.
3. Turn on the machine and select the FROZEN JUICE preset. Let it process until complete.
4. Once ready (indicated by three beeps), pour the slush into glasses and serve.

*Nutritional Value (per serving)*

Calories: ~80 | Carbohydrates: 20g | Sugar: 18g | Protein: 0g | Fat: 0g | Fiber: 0g

Mango Frozen Juice Slush

*Ingredients*

- 2 cups of mango juice drink (any brand)
- 1-2 teaspoons honey or agave syrup (optional, for sweetness)

**Prep:** 5 minutes

**Servings**: 2

*Instructions*

1. Chill the mango juice drink in the refrigerator for 10–15 minutes.
2. Pour the chilled mango drink into the Ninja Slushi machine's vessel. Add honey/agave syrup, if using.
3. Turn on the machine, select the FROZEN JUICE preset, and let it process.
4. Once the slush is ready (signaled by three beeps), pour into glasses and serve immediately.

### Nutritional Value (per serving)

Calories: ~70 | Carbohydrates: 17g | Sugar: 15g | Protein: 0g | Fat: 0g | Fiber: 0g

Berry Frozen Juice Slush

### Ingredients

- 2 cups of mixed berry fruit drink (any brand)
- 1-2 teaspoons honey or agave syrup (optional, for sweetness)

**Prep:** 5 minutes

**Servings**: 2

### Instructions

1. Place the berry fruit drink in the refrigerator for 10–15 minutes to chill.
2. Pour the chilled drink into the Ninja Slushi machine's vessel and add honey or agave syrup, if desired.
3. Turn on the machine and select the FROZEN JUICE preset. Allow it to process.
4. Once the slush is ready (indicated by three beeps), pour into glasses and serve immediately.

### Nutritional Value (per serving)

Calories: ~50 | Carbohydrates: 12g | Sugar: 10g | Protein: 0g | Fat: 0g | Fiber: 0g

# Orange Pineapple Frozen Juice Slush

## Ingredients

- 2 cups of orange pineapple juice (from any brand)
- 1-2 teaspoons honey or agave syrup (optional, for sweetness)

**Prep:** 5 minutes

**Servings**: 2

## Instructions

1. Place the orange pineapple juice in the refrigerator for 10–15 minutes to chill.
2. Pour the chilled juice into the Ninja Slushi machine's vessel. Add honey or agave syrup, if desired.
3. Turn on the machine, select the FROZEN JUICE preset, and let it process.
4. Once the slush is ready (indicated by three beeps), pour into glasses and serve immediately.

## Nutritional Value (per serving)

Calories: ~60 | Carbohydrates: 14g | Sugar: 12g | Protein: 0g | Fat: 0g | Fiber: 0g

# Raspberry Frozen Juice Slush

## Ingredients

- 2 cups of raspberry juice drink (from any brand)
- 1-2 teaspoons honey or agave syrup (optional, for sweetness)

**Prep:** 5 minutes

**Servings**: 2

*Instructions*

1. Chill the raspberry juice drink in the refrigerator for 10–15 minutes.
2. Pour the chilled juice into the Ninja Slushi machine's vessel. Add honey or agave syrup, if desired.
3. Turn on the machine, select the FROZEN JUICE preset, and let it process.
4. Once the slush is ready (indicated by three beeps), pour into glasses and serve immediately.

*Nutritional Value (per serving)*

Calories: ~60 | Carbohydrates: 14g | Sugar: 11g | Protein: 0g | Fat: 0g | Fiber: 0g

Cherry Frozen Juice Slush

*Ingredients*

- 2 cups of cherry fruit drink (from any brand)
- 1-2 teaspoons honey or agave syrup (optional, for sweetness)

**Prep**: 5 minutes

**Servings**: 2

*Instructions*

1. Refrigerate the cherry fruit drink for 10–15 minutes to ensure it starts cold.
2. Pour the chilled cherry drink into the Ninja Slushi vessel. If desired, add honey or agave syrup for a touch of extra sweetness.
3. Turn on the machine and select the FROZEN JUICE preset. Let it run until the slushie is ready (the machine will beep three times).
4. Dispense into glasses and enjoy.

*Nutritional Value (per serving)*

Calories: ~55 | Carbohydrates: 13g | Sugar: 11g | Protein: 0g | Fat: 0g | Fiber: 0g

Apple Frozen Juice Slush

*Ingredients*

- 2 cups of apple fruit drink (any brand)
- 1-2 teaspoons honey or agave syrup (optional, for sweetness)

**Prep:** 5 minutes

**Servings**: 2

*Instructions*

1. Chill the apple fruit drink in the refrigerator for 10–15 minutes.
2. Pour the chilled drink into the Ninja Slushi vessel, adding honey or agave syrup if desired.
3. Turn on the machine, select the FROZEN JUICE preset, and let it process.
4. Once the slush is ready (indicated by three beeps), pour into glasses and enjoy.

*Nutritional Value (per serving)*

Calories: ~50 | Carbohydrates: 13g | Sugar: 10g | Protein: 0g | Fat: 0g | Fiber: 0g

Tangerine Frozen Juice Slush

*Ingredients*

- 2 cups of tangerine juice (from any brand)
- 1-2 teaspoons honey or agave syrup (optional, for added sweetness)

**Prep:** 5 minutes

**Servings**: 2

*Instructions*

1. Chill the tangerine juice in the refrigerator for 10-15 minutes.
2. Pour the chilled juice into the Ninja Slushi machine's vessel. Add honey or agave syrup if desired.
3. Turn on the machine and select the FROZEN JUICE preset. Let it process.
4. Once the slush is ready (indicated by three beeps), pour into glasses and serve.

*Nutritional Value (per serving)*

Calories: ~60 |Carbohydrates: 14g | Sugar: 12g | Protein: 0g | Fat: 0g | Fiber: 0g

## Lemonade Frozen Juice Slush

### Ingredients

- 2 cups of lemonade drink (any brand)
- 1-2 teaspoons honey or agave syrup (optional, for sweetness)

**Prep:** 5 minutes

**Servings**: 2

### Instructions

1. Chill the lemonade drink in the refrigerator for 10–15 minutes.
2. Pour the chilled lemonade into the Ninja Slushi vessel. Add honey or agave syrup, if desired.
3. Turn on the machine and select the FROZEN JUICE preset. Let the machine process the drink.
4. Once the slush is ready (indicated by three beeps), pour into glasses to enjoy.

*Nutritional Value (per serving)*

Calories: ~60 | Carbohydrates: 14g | Sugar: 12g | Protein: 0g | Fat: 0g | Fiber: 0g

# Peach Frozen Juice Slush

## Ingredients

- 2 cups of peach fruit drink (from any brand)
- 1-2 teaspoons honey or agave syrup (optional, for sweetness)

**Prep:** 5 minutes

**Servings**: 2

## Instructions

1. Chill the peach fruit drink in the refrigerator for 10-15 minutes.
2. Pour the chilled drink into the Ninja Slushi vessel. Add honey or agave syrup if desired.
3. Turn on the machine and select the FROZEN JUICE preset. Let the machine process it.
4. Once the machine beeps three times, pour the slush into glasses and serve.

## Nutritional Value (per serving)

Calories: ~50 | Carbohydrates: 13g | Sugar: 10g | Protein: 0g | Fat: 0g | Fiber: 0g

# Dragon Fruit Frozen Juice Slush

## Ingredients

- 2 cups of dragon fruit drink (from any brand)
- 1-2 tablespoons of water (for adjusting thickness)

**Prep:** 5 minutes

**Servings**: 2

## Instructions

1. Put the dragon fruit drink in the refrigerator to chill for 10-15 minutes.
2. Pour chilled drink into the Ninja slushi vessel and add the bit of water to help blend the mixture.
3. Turn on the machine, select the FROZEN JUICE preset, and let it process.
4. Once the slush is ready (the machine will beep three times), pour into glasses and serve immediately.

## Nutritional Value (per serving)

Calories: ~60 | Carbohydrates: 15g | Sugar: 13g | Protein: 0g | Fat: 0g | Fiber: 0g

# Keeping IT in Top Shape

Keeping your Ninja Slushi maker in top shape ensures that it continues to deliver perfectly slushy drinks every time you use it. Proper care and maintenance not only extend the life of the machine but also ensure the best performance. Here are some tips to help you maintain your Ninja Slushi maker:

1. Avoid Overfilling

Overfilling the blending vessel can cause spills or impact the efficiency of the machine. Stick to the recommended ingredient amounts for best results.

2. Use the Right Ingredients

The machine works best with well-chilled ingredients. Avoid putting hard frozen items, like large chunks of ice, directly into the machine as this may put strain on the motor. Always use chilled liquids or pre-frozen ingredients for optimal slushy texture.

3. Regular Cleaning After Each Use

Dispense Remaining Drink: With the machine running, dispense any remaining slush, then stop the program by pressing the Program button.

Quick Rinse: Press the Rinse button, fill the vessel with water to remove any leftover drink, and dispense it out.

Deep Clean: For a deeper clean, add a drop or two of dish soap to the vessel, rinse for a minute, and then dispose of the soapy water. Press the Rinse button again to stop the cycle.

Clean Removable Parts: Unlock the bale handle, remove the vessel, and detach the auger from the evaporator. Wipe the evaporator with a damp cloth (don't use abrasive materials like steel wool or harsh chemical cleaners. These can scratch the surfaces and damage the machine), clean the condensation catch, and wash the drip tray and cover either by hand or in the dishwasher (avoid the heated dry cycle).

Wipe Down the Base: Finally, wipe down the motor base and evaporator. Allow all parts to dry before reassembling. Ensure the base is dry before plugging it back in to avoid any electrical damage.

4. Proper Storage

Store in a dry place: Always store the Ninja Slushi maker in a clean, dry area when not in use to prevent dust and debris from collecting on the unit.

Avoid direct sunlight or heat: Direct exposure to sunlight or heat sources can warp the plastic and degrade the machine's components over time.

5. Troubleshooting

If you notice the machine is not functioning properly, such as producing uneven textures or strange noises, it may be due to a clog or an issue with the motor. Always troubleshoot using the manual's suggestions and, if necessary, contact customer service for assistance.

# Measurement Conversion Chart

## Dry Measurements Chart

| Measurement | Equivalent |
|---|---|
| 1 cup | 240 ml |
| 1 tablespoon | 15 ml |
| 1 teaspoon | 5 ml |
| 1 ounce | 28.35 grams |
| 1 pound | 453.59 grams |

## Volume

| Milliliters (ml) | Teaspoons |
|---|---|
| 5 mL | 1 teaspoon |
| 15 mL | 3 teaspoons |
| 30 mL | 6 teaspoons |
| 60 mL | 12 teaspoons |
| 120 mL | 24 teaspoons |

## Oven Temperatures

| Measurement | Equivalent |
|---|---|
| 1 cup | 240 ml |
| 1 tablespoon | 15 ml |
| 1 teaspoon | 5 ml |
| 1 ounce | 28.35 grams |
| 1 pound | 453.59 grams |

## Baking in Grams

| Measurement | Equivalent |
|---|---|
| 1 cup | 120 grams |
| 1 tablespoon | 15 grams |
| 1 teaspoon | 5 grams |
| 1 ounce | 28.35 grams |
| 1 pound | 453.59 grams |

## Liquid Conversion

| Measurement | Equivalent |
|---|---|
| 1 cup | 240 ml |
| 1 fluid ounce | 29.57 ml |
| 1 pint | 473.18 ml |
| 1 quart | 946.35 ml |
| 1 gallon | 3,785.41 ml |

## Weight

| Pounds | Kilograms (kg) |
|---|---|
| 1 pound | 0.4536 kg |
| 2 pounds | 0.9072 kg |
| 5 pounds | 2.268 kg |
| 10 pounds | 4.536 kg |
| 20 pounds | 9.072 kg |

# A short message from the author

Hey there! How's the book treating you? I'm super curious to know what you think about it! Your thoughts can really make a difference.

Could you spare just a minute to jot down a quick review on Amazon? Even a few sentences would mean the world!

Simply click the link 🔗 or scan the QR code below and scroll down to get to the *'Write a customer review'* button to leave your review on Amazon

🔗 rebrand.ly/slush/LM

QR code

Thank you for taking the time to share your thoughts!

Made in the USA
Monee, IL
22 December 2024

75117816R00070